A *NEW YORK TIMES* BESTSELLER

An Official Selection from Emma Watson's International
Book Club, Our Shared Shelf

Named a Best Book of the Year by NPR, *GQ*, *Time*,
The Globe and Mail, *Financial Times*, *Library Journal*,
BuzzFeed, *BookPage*, *NYLON*, *Electric Literature*,
Entropy, and *Bustle*

Selected as a Best Book of the Year by the New York Public
Library and the Chicago Public Library

A *New York Times* Editors' Choice

A Barnes & Noble Discover Great New Writers Selection

An American Booksellers Association Indie Next Selection

"A luminous, poetic memoir." —*Entertainment Weekly*

"Sometimes a writer's voice is so distinctive, so angry and messy
yet wise, that her story takes on the kind of urgency that makes
you turn pages faster and faster. Terese Marie Mailhot has one of
those voices." —ANGELA LEDGERWOOD, *Esquire*

"Powerful and raw, *Heart Berries* looks unflinchingly at trauma,
love, pain, self-acceptance, and what it means to be a Native
woman today." —JARRY LEE, *BuzzFeed*

"This gut punch of a memoir . . . [is] essentially
a love letter, full of humor and truth, to tough, challenging
women everywhere." —*Marie Claire*

"*Heart Berries* is a bruising story, purposefully intense, dark and yet light-filled, in which the act of cleaning is a distraction from pain and also a memorialization of suffering." —*Literary Hub*

"Mailhot's memoir isn't just another confession of the hells of living with PTSD and BiPolar disorder: it's a woman writing herself out of the darkness and into acceptance of the events in her life." —*The Coil*

"Her poetic memoir is painfully straight to the point—in the best way possible. It's a pleasure to read along as she takes control of her life and finds her voice." —*HelloGiggles*

"*Heart Berries* is a poetic, coming-of-age memoir told through essays that explore everything from motherhood and daughter-hood, to love and loss, to family and identity, to the intersections of art and mental illness, and more. Above all, perhaps, it is a story about women telling stories—the power of women speaking (or writing) hard truths about their lives." —*Bustle*

"In an age when memoirs are all the rage (for better or worse), this one stands out . . . Somehow, [Mailhot] has found the words—most unusual ones—to tell her story, and because she uses words in such strange ways, the result is spooky and powerful . . . A roller coaster of a read, and perhaps one especially valuable for those who have struggled with mental illness and/or obsessive love." —*Star-Tribune* (Minneapolis)

"Mailhot asks us as readers to push beyond our outworn notions concerning female experience, mental illness, motherhood, and more, in order to inhabit that transcendent ambiguity and complexity she reaches . . . *Heart Berries* takes us on a tour of these very confounding complications and we're richer for it." —*Kenyon Review*

"Searing . . . A harrowing story of illness, loss, and abuse, as well as the restorative power of writing one's story and having it recognized by others."   —*Public Books*

"In gorgeous prose and with searing honesty, she shares her fight for both love and independence."   —*Read It Forward*

"Mailhot works language like a poet and lets memory and time twist around to elicit from herself deeper truths about childhood trauma, mental illness, Native identity, love, romance, and motherhood."   —*Pasatiempo*

"In the poetic essays that compose this memoir, Terese Marie Mailhot examines coming of age on the Seabird Island Indian Reservation in the Pacific Northwest; post traumatic stress disorder and bipolar II disorder; memorializing her mother; reconciling with her father; and more."   —*Autostraddle*

"Her story is surprising and illuminating, pushing away from traditional narratives and expected boundaries . . . Her own gift is the ability to speak the truth without fear of consequence." —*Guernica*

"*Heart Berries* shook me to my core. It wasn't just the emotionally jarring, painful experiences shared by author Terese Marie Mailhot . . . but also by her unembellished, electric prose."
                              —*Inlander*

"Brief but mighty."   —*THE Magazine*

"Presenting herself at times as 'ruined'—and 'ruining'—she radiates a vulnerability that Fields's deft narration captures. Mailhot's questions and answers at the audiobook's end are especially enlightening; listeners may want to listen once through, then loop back a second time to fully absorb her intimate honesty."   —*AudioFile*

"In this poetic memoir of remarkable lyric power, debut author Terese Marie Mailhot blends a deeply personal narrative with fierce (and often funny) political consciousness in sentences so lean that reading them smarts . . . The immense hurt in this book cannot dim the steady beam of Mailhot's brilliance. *Heart Berries* is a triumph to relish." —*The Riveter*

"Through this beautifully written memoir we get glimpses, snapshots and explicit details of her experience . . . It goes without saying *Heart Berries* is necessary today." —Rebel Women Lit

"In these 11 essays, Mailhot takes readers on her journey toward personal truth: a messy, revelatory process reflected both in the book's narrative structure and its searing, poetic language . . . A lyrical work from a remarkable new author, *Heart Berries* is a triumph." —*The Gazette* (Iowa)

"This book is ache and balm. It is electric honesty and rigorous craft. It concerns a woman who veers into difficult and haunted corners. She meets ghosts and hospitals. She ends up in a mutinous wing of memoir, disobeying all colonial postures, 'neat narratives,' formulas, and governments. The resulting story is brave and bewitching. I am so grateful to Terese Marie Mailhot, a fiery new voice, whose words devoured my heart."

—KYO MACLEAR, bestselling author of *Birds Art Life*

"There is some word we have not invented yet that means honesty to the hundredth power, that means courage, exponentially extended, that means I will flay myself for my art, for my survival, for my family, to keep breathing, to keep writing, to keep being alive. Inside that opening is beauty beyond all measure, the truth that art was invented to carry, and power enough to light the word. This book is that kind of opening."

—PAM HOUSTON, author of *Contents May Have Shifted*

"*Heart Berries* makes me think of a quote I have always loved: 'Beauty is truth, truth beauty' (Keats). With a keen eye for intense truth and thoroughly crafted beauty, Mailhot's debut sings like poetry, and stays with you long after you've finished the last page."

—KATHERENA VERMETTE,
award-winning author of *The Break*

"*Heart Berries* is phenomenal. I finished the book and went right back to the beginning to read through once again; my understanding deepened, as did the mystery. Mailhot's voice is so clear, so disruptive, so assured, and always so mesmerizingly poetic—it somehow startles and lulls all at once. I was KNOCKED DOWN."

—JUSTIN TORRES, author of *We the Animals*

"Unearthing medicine and receiving power requires you to give your life, and in her debut memoir, Mailhot fearlessly delivers. By turns tender, sad, angry, and funny, *Heart Berries* is a thought-provoking, powerful exploration of what it means to be a contemporary Indigenous woman and mother."

—EDEN ROBINSON, author of the Scotiabank Giller Prize short-listed novel *Son of a Trickster*

"In this debut memoir, Terese Marie Mailhot sends across generations a love letter to women considered difficult. She sends a manifesto toward remembering—culture and heartbreak and laughter. She writes to the men who love these women. She writes prose tight as a perfect sheet, tucked . . . To read this book is to engage with one of our very best minds at work."

—TONI JENSEN, author of *From the Hilltop*

"This stunning, poetic memoir from Terese Marie Mailhot burns like hot coal. I read it in a single feverish session, completely absorbed and transported by Mailhot's powerful and original voice . . . The strength of her writing comes from Mailhot's fearless embrace of emotional darkness and in her depiction of the psychic cost of living in a white man's world." —*BookPage*

"Mailhot fearlessly addresses intimately personal issues with a scorching honesty derived from psychological pain and true epiphany . . . Slim, elegiac, and delivered with an economy of meticulous prose, the book calibrates the author's history as an abused child and an adult constantly at war with the demons of mental illness. An elegant, deeply expressive meditation infused with humanity and grace." —*Kirkus Reviews*

"Mailhot's first book defies containment and categorization. In titled essays, it is a poetic memoir told in otherworldly sentences . . . Not shy, nor raw, nor typical in any way, this is a powerfully crafted and vulnerable account of living and writing about it." —*Booklist*

HEART
BERRIES

A Memoir

TERESE MARIE
MAILHOT

COUNTERPOINT
BERKELEY, CALIFORNIA

Heart Berries

The Library of Congress has cataloged the hardcover as follows:
Names: Mailhot, Terese Marie, author.
Title: Heart berries : a memoir / Terese Marie Mailhot.
Description: Berkeley, CA : Counterpoint Press, [2018]
Identifiers: LCCN 2017051069 | ISBN 9781619023345
Subjects: LCSH: Mailhot, Terese Marie—Health. | Post-traumatic stress disorder—Patients—Northwest, Pacific—Biography. | Manic-depressive illness—Patients—Northwest, Pacific—Biography. | Indian women—Northwest, Pacific—Biography.
Classification: LCC RC552.P67 M3555 2018 | DDC 362.19685/210092 [B] —dc23
LC record available at https://lccn.loc.gov/2017051069

Paperback ISBN: 978-1-64009-160-3

Cover design by Donna Cheng
Book design by Wah-Ming Chang

COUNTERPOINT
2560 Ninth Street, Suite 318
Berkeley, CA 94710
www.counterpointpress.com

Printed in the United States of America
Distributed by Publishers Group West

10 9 8 7 6 5 4 3 2 1

For Karen Joyce Bobb (Wahzinak)

I want you to know, if you ever read this, there was a time when I would rather have had you by my side than any one of these words; I would rather have had you by my side than all the blue in the world.

—MAGGIE NELSON

Contents

HEART
BERRIES

1

INDIAN CONDITION

My story was maltreated. The words were too wrong and ugly to speak. I tried to tell someone my story, but he thought it was a hustle. He marked it as solicitation. The man took me shopping with his pity. I was silenced by charity—like so many Indians. I kept my hand out. My story became the hustle.

Women asked me what my endgame was. I hadn't thought about it. I considered marrying one of the men and sitting with my winnings, but I was too smart to sit. I took their money and went to school. I was hungry and took more. When I gained the faculty to speak my story, I realized I had given men too much.

The thing about women from the river is that our currents are endless. We sometimes outrun ourselves. I stopped answering men's questions or their calls.

Women asked me for my story.

My grandmother told me about Jesus. We knelt to pray. She told me to close my eyes. It was the only thing she asked me to do properly. She had conviction, but she also taught me to be mindless. We started recipes and lost track. We forgot ingredients. Our cakes never rose. We started an applehead doll—the shrunken, carved head sat on a bookshelf years after she left.

When she died nobody noticed me. Indian girls can be forgotten so well they forget themselves.

My mother brought healers to our home, and I thought she was trying to exorcise me—a little ghost. Psychics came. Our house was still ruptured. I started to craft ideas. I wrapped myself in a Pendleton blanket and picked blueberries. I pretended I was ancient. A healer looked at me. He was tall and his jeans were dirty.

He knelt down. I thought I was in trouble, so I told him that I had been good. He said, "You don't need to be nice."

My mother said that was when I became trouble.

That's when my nightmares came. A spinning wheel, a white porcelain tooth, a snarling mouth, and lightning haunted me. My mother told me they were visions.

"Turn your shirt backward to confuse the ghosts," she said, and sent me to bed.

My mother insisted that I embrace my power. On my first day of school I bound myself a small book. The teacher complimented my vocabulary, and my mother told me school was *a choice*.

She fed me traditional food. I went to bed early every night, but I never slept well.

I fell ill with tuberculosis. Mother brought back the healers. I told them my grandmother was speaking to me.

Zohar, a white mystic, a tarot reader, told me she spoke to spirits, too. "Your grandmother says she misses you," she said.

"We could never make a cake," I said.

"She was just telling me that. What ingredient did you usually forget?"

I knew this was a test, but a strange one, because she didn't speak to my grandmother either. I remember my mother was watching us, holding her breath.

"Eggs," I said.

My spiritual fraud distanced my grandmother's spirit from me. It became harder to stomach myself, and harder to eat.

"Does that happen to you?" I asked.

"What?" Zohar asked.

"Did you ever want to stop eating?"

"No," she said.

Zohar asked my mother if she could sleep next to my bed, on the floor. She listened to me all night. Storytelling. What potential there was in being awful. My mindlessness became a gift. I didn't feel compelled to tell any moral tales or ancient ones. I learned how story was always meant to be for Indian women: immediate and necessary and fearless, like all good lies.

My story was maltreated. I was a teenager when I got married. I wanted a safe home. Despair isn't a conduit for love. We ruined each other, and then my mother died. I had to leave the reservation. I had to get my GED. I left my home because welfare made me choose between necessities. I used a check and some cash I saved for a ticket away—and knew I would arrive with a deficit. That's when I started to illustrate my story and when it became a means of survival. The ugly truth is that I lost my son Isadore in court. The Hague Convention. The ugly of *that* truth is that I gave birth to my second son as I was losing my first. My court date and my delivery aligned. In the hospital, they told me that my first son would go with his father.

"What about this boy," I said, with Isaiah in my arms.

"They don't seem interested yet," my lawyer said.

I brought Isaiah home from the hospital, and then packed Isadore's bag. My ex-husband Vito took him, along with police escorts. Before they left, I asked Vito if he wanted to hold his new baby. I don't know why I offered, but he didn't kiss our baby or tell him goodbye. He didn't say he was sorry, or that it was unfortunate. Who wants one boy and not another?

It's too ugly—to speak this story. It sounds like a beggar. How could misfortune follow me so well, and why did I choose it every time?

I learned how to make a honey reduction of the ugly sentences. Still, my voice cracks.

I packed my baby and left my reservation. I came from the mountains to an infinite and flat brown to bury my grief. I left because I was hungry.

In my first writing classes, my professor told me that the human condition was misery. I'm a river widened by misery, and the potency of my language is more than human. It's an Indian condition to be proud of survival but reluctant to call it resilience. Resilience seems ascribed to a human conditioning in white people.

The Indian condition is my grandmother. She was a nursery teacher. There are stories that she brought children to our kitchen, gave them laxatives, and then put newspaper on the ground. She squatted before them and made faces to illustrate how hard they should push. She dewormed children this way, and she learned that in residential school—where parasites and nuns and priests contaminated generations of our people. Indians froze trying to run away, and many starved. Nuns and priests ran out of places to put bones, so they built us into the walls of new boarding schools.

I can see Grandmother's face in front of those children. Her hands felt like rose petals, and her eyes were soft and round like buttons. She liked carnations and canned milk. She transcended resilience and actualized what Indians weren't taught to know: We are unmovable. Time seems measured by grief and anticipatory grief. I don't think she even measured time.

2

HEART BERRIES

You had a hard-on for my oratory. Some of my stories were fabricated. I had authority—a thing that people like you haven't witnessed. It comes from a traditional upbringing and regarding my work as something more sacred than generations of effort or study. It's something on a continuum, so far reaching you know it came from an inhuman place. Story *is* inhuman and beyond me, and I'm not sure you ever recognized that. You knew to be excited in proximity to my power.

We started the affair in a small booth at Village Inn. I didn't sleep the night before. You were my teacher, and we discussed my fiction. My work was skeletal, before you. I waited for the right silence and then said flatly that I liked you.

"Do we get a hotel?" you said.

Your hands were shaking. I reached out and touched them—they were double mine and whiter.

I knew, before I was close to you, that your cotton-blue hoodie smelled like smoke, and I could put my entire body beneath it. I knew that your skin wasn't rough. I knew that I was not going to be the same person for loving you.

We went back to our respective lives. We agreed to talk about it sometime soon. It was winter. I wore a brown corduroy jacket most days, and I remember waiting to be with you—putting my fingers in the jacket pockets until the pockets couldn't contain my incessant want. My fingers felt swollen with focus and desire. I remember pulling threads, looking in the mirror, and seeing myself how you might see me. New.

While I waited, I went on a trip with a man I barely liked. You didn't call for two days. He insisted on sleeping in the same bed in our cabin. Our room had a skylight. I couldn't enjoy anything without acknowledging he was in the room. I tried to bathe alone and he played a guitar on the other side of the door. I was bored and asked for horses.

"What?" he said.

"I want to be on a horse," I said.

We were somewhere mountainous, and it was snowing. He spent the morning calling stalls and asking for rates. He seemed offended when I told him I needed a warmer sweater, matching gloves, and that the breakfast we had wasn't right. And that I might need wool socks as well. He seemed surprised that I was not fun loving.

I was rude and gratuitous. I went horseback riding with the man. He was almost jaundiced—he was so sick in love with me. I wanted as much of the world as I could take, and I didn't have the conscience to be ashamed.

You messaged me when I was playing slots with the man. You messaged that you had left your girlfriend, for me. You asked me how soon we could meet. I told the man I was ready to go home. It was urgent. He planned to go ice-skating, but I said no. He planned a tour of a haunted house, but I said no.

The man I had been conditioning was not happy with me. He knew something was wrong, and that's when I wondered if maybe falling in love looked like a crisis to an observer.

You had a jawline, and I wanted to crawl under your gaze—under your chin. I was desirous to be beneath you.

The first few nights you tell me things.

"I'd burn my life down for you," you said.

There was still so much to tell you—things too ugly to know or say.

I wanted to know what I looked like to you. A sin committed and a prayer answered, you said.

You looked like a hamburger fried in a donut. You were hairy and large. Falling in love felt fluid. It snowed when we fell in love. Everything reminded me of warm milk. Everything seemed less real. I thought my cup was overflowing. I found myself caressing my own face.

My son and I let you visit. I told him my friend was coming. He put on a Batman costume and hid behind the couch until you came.

"When is he coming?" Isaiah said.

"Any minute."

When you arrived, Isaiah sprung out and stood quietly. You let him be weird. He was seven, and his fingers were perpetually sticky. My son was a smaller bolt of lightning—uncontained and sweeter than me. You were patient with him, and I watched you both put together a Lego set.

Safety wasn't familiar—not with men. Our life felt brighter together.

We started to argue about autonomy and the agency I lacked with you. Neither one of us could pull away, so things erupted. Both of us had jobs and commitments. Our lives became less productive when productivity was pivotal.

Your agent called. I was underneath your chin, burying my nose into your chest and searching with my hands. You finally sold your book. Your neighbors had horses and chickens, but the land was insufficiently small. The place always smelled like manure but not in the worst of winter. Scents can freeze.

So many things were signs. The Spanish radio station you put on during our drives. You said you were "trying to immerse yourself in the language."

I sunk into myself. I knew better. White people are brutally awkward, even you.

You didn't pamper me like the men I had conditioned. You didn't jump to buy things. You thought of us as equals. You expected me to do things and wondered why I wanted everything on the menu. You didn't take out your wallet and tell me who I was. Those moments never came.

You ruined me with touch. It was a different exploitation.

You asked me for my secret. I told you about the son who didn't live with me. I told you that I lock myself in the bathroom to cry when I remember his milk breath. I knew what it felt like to sleep next to him in bed, and he was just gone. I told you I go away.

You said you'd be on the other side of the door. That's how perfect love is at first. Solutions are simple, and problems are laid out simply.

I knew that the way I had been living was too complicated for you to see up close. I should have consulted a healer before I went further with you.

Our culture is based in the profundity things carry. We're always trying to see the world the way our ancestors did—we feel less of a relationship to the natural world. There was a time when we dictated our beliefs and told ourselves what was real, or what was wrong or right. There weren't any abstractions. We knew that our language came before the world.

I knew I was not well. I thought of the first healer, who was just a boy. My friend Denise told me the story. She called him Heart Berry Boy, or O'dimin. His name means "strawberry" in the language. Denise and I struggled and came up together—she named her son after the boy. The people in his village were sick and dying because the Indian world was shifting. The boy lost his mother. O'dimin became a sorrowful kid who found solace in the dream world. He fell asleep and spun a restlessness that comes when people are waiting to die. Sometimes grief is a nothing feeling.

The spirits finally came to him in a dream and told him to leave the village. He asked the elders what he should do, and they told him their own dreams, and that he should introduce himself by name and lineage to a bear and follow her until she gave him a gift.

He walked alone in the valley, and, when Bear presented herself, she stood tall. They looked at each other. He followed her. She sunk her paws into wet dirt, and then he told her his name. She started to feel sick. Her heaving seemed bloody and reminded him of his mother. Bear told him she was not his mother. She told him to let her rest, but he didn't.

She said, "I can't unearth this medicine and give you power unless you give your life to this." She was willing to die to keep her secrets from weak people.

He sat with her. She put her claws into a strawberry patch and produced ripe berries. She ate and slept. He collected some berries and brought them to the people. Eventually, he started to plant and show others what he learned. This was how the first medicine man came to be.

♥

I learned that any power asks you to dedicate your life to its expansion. Things feel continuous when I think of my gifts and heritage. With you, things don't feel right sometimes. I believe you obstruct my healing.

What I notice with you is that I look outside whenever I'm close to a window, and I wonder how many women feel that way. I feel things I would rather feel alone.

Things have become more real with you. Every time I start to cry, you tell me that you can't keep me from leaving. I feel abject without your passion. I feel uncontrollable with you.

In bed, daylight breaks through our tented sheets. I see you, Casey. You will always love me in a shadow. It's not torturous to be with you when I consider being without. Instead of feeling the gasping pain of my powerlessness, I straddle it and put your hands on my breasts. I tell you that I'd burn my life down for you.

We try to remember each other this way, and I'm not sure how many times I can do this to you before I forget myself. I want you to will my pain away. I try to think that the things I do to you, I won't ever do harder to someone else.

I guess heartbreak is simple. Problems seem to unfurl themselves like crumpled bills on a nightstand.

The first night that I locked myself away, you didn't even notice I was gone. Every door is the same when I kneel in a corner—with a hand over my mouth. Every bathroom floor is different, but no mourning I do feels familiar. It feels brand new.

3

INDIAN SICK

Casey,
I want to be polite and present myself as decent. I know the math of regret and nostalgia. I regret leaving you, and I'm disappointed you let me go.

I don't remember what I did. I know that I cried next to you, and I was wearing lingerie. You were angry with me for wanting to die—more than that, you were upset that I was weak minded. I was dramatic and unhinged. I couldn't placate. I know that's what I should have done.

I remember that I was wearing black lace and new stockings. I wasn't stable, but men don't usually care about that. I didn't perform. I found myself uncovered and vulnerable, in fabric so thin—I thought of everything I've belted against my flesh and unclasped again and again.

You used me. I know you think animals are sentient. You treat your dog well. I needed to talk to you. The way we operate asks a lot from me before I can ask something of you.

This letter can spiral out of control like me, and maybe you won't read it, because I might fail to send it, or you might decide your life without me is worth maintaining. You have white sensibilities, and who can fault you for being practical? I'd like this letter to be ashamed and wild like me, and I'd like to know you read it and wanted me more.

I told the staff this is my journal.

I'm going to die an Indian death. I want to lay my neck on the cool steel alloy of the train tracks back home. I want the death of a rez dog. Mutts can't keep away from the tracks.

I'm writing you from a behavioral health service building. I agreed to commit myself under the condition they would let me write. You should have thought before you made a crazy Indian woman your lover. Feel culpable in my insanity because you are partly to blame.

I am not good, but you knew that. Why think less of me in here? You're so economic with your language and your time. I understand your frustration with me. You want to spare yourself any tax or energy, and I am acutely aware of my impulsivity. It might be all the same to you. Do you still love me? I still want you. Don't think less of me for being crazy. Don't think that I am the only one culpable in my craziness.

I was walking through the house in the dark. I had covered the windows and mirrors. I was just unseeing things, dragging my feet along the wood panels until I found myself in the kitchen. I could not forget the familiarity of the kitchen or its drawers and instruments.

Keep in mind you were once desperate for me. I need help, and I cannot stop thinking that every transgression has brought me closer to a light, a striking beacon that tells me death is absolution. I have never chosen light.

Do you consider me a transgression?

I'm tired of the constant stories and the truth I don't acknowledge. They're not medicine anymore. I'm not medicine anymore. The words are flaccid, and the things I used to find sacred are torment. I'm stepping into my own undertow. My own valley is closing in on me. I curl into walls, ashamed at my cowardice. I am sick or possessed.

The spirits used to possess the people. We called it "Indian sick," and it was the first illness to be accounted for. It begins with want, with taking, and ends with a silence that hurts and makes us beg. There were stories about the cures and causes. Women tried to eat soapberries, or nothing, and talked about how we all had it coming. When the first children died it was too late to stop talking. When the beings took the women they bound them in blood. They were buried in wombs of sad memory. The only thing, the right thing—the thing that brought about our immunity—was the knowledge that something instinctual would carry us back. The awareness that our ancestors were watching was vital. I don't feel the eyes of my grandmother anymore.

What I feel struck with is something smaller, in a less impressive world. I woke up today, confused, inside of something feminine and ancestral in its misery. I woke up as the bones of my ancestors locked in government storage. My illness has carried me into white buildings, into the doctor's office and the therapist's—with nothing to say, other than I need my grandmother's eyes on me, smiling at my misguided heart. Imagine their faces when I say that?

At the behavioral health service building, I felt something: a young woman staring at me. She was soft-looking and crazy-eyed, sitting with an old, gray, wool blanket in her lap. Avoiding her stare was the first task I failed at in the institution.

"You're pretty," she said.

"Thank you," I said.

"No," she said. "Thank *you*."

Scared, I smiled and nodded. We both looked out of place, and, when I considered what kind of woman would look like she belonged here, I drew a blank.

"I got these moles," she said, and pointed to the five surrounding her mouth. "They're spitballs from Jesus."

It was a mistake to check myself in. So many people said something wasn't right. I told them you were my savior, and this is what neglect can do. They didn't believe me—it's important to be loved back. No matter, I'm a mother. My son will stay with a friend. Do this, they said. *Something is wrong*, I know.

We passed the hours in the waiting room watching the Weather Channel. We watched tornadoes and the fury of water wash around. Slowly, women were called in for assessment with psychiatrists and then more women came in to wait.

I was eventually alone on the couch. Regular to crazy-looking—I was somewhere in the middle, wearing an oversize black petticoat and a too-red lipstick. There was a glass where workers observed us, and I recognized a man on the other side, Josue. Years before, we worked at a call center together. We had lunch a few times, and he told me about his night shifts at a hospital. He came outside and observed me in a quiet and careful way. Observation is a skill. Observation isn't easy, and the right eyes can make me feel like a deer, while the wrong ones make me feel like a monster.

He stood in front of me with a binder in his hands.

"Terese," he said.

"No. Don't do this," I said.

He smiled. "It's good you're here."

I said a lot of things to fill a silence. He didn't want to know why I was there. I told him every reason except the truth. He was kind of a dick, in that it didn't matter what I said. He just smiled and sat with me for a moment and then went back to work.

A nurse came in with a girl who couldn't have been older than eighteen.

"Sit," the nurse said.

"Calm your tits," the young girl said, turning to me. "Wild night?"

The fuzz of the couch came off in my hand. The orange fur of it was familiar. A nurse came out of a gray door and motioned for me. I followed her into a room. She left me there with the door cracked. There was an urge to leap and run. The doctor walked in. She was petite and wore a blush hijab, with wine-colored lipstick.

"On a scale of one to ten, how bad is your depression?"

"Seven," I said.

"Seven's not a ten." She smiled. "Why are you here?"

"This is the last thing I can do."

"Do you have a plan to hurt yourself?"

"It's dramatic. I don't think it's a real plan," I said.

She sat up straighter.

"I think things would be better if I was dead."

She told me there was a better solution to pain, and that she's seen it herself. She asked me to stay for five days. I'd be out two days before Christmas. I had already bought my son's gifts. I asked her if I could write. She said yes. I asked her if I would be out before Christmas *for sure*. She said yes.

"Do this program for you," she said.

The forms made me feel big. My signature mattered. I was signing a new treaty. The gamut of questions and searches through my bag lasted for hours, and, during that time, several nurses pointed out that things do, in fact, get better.

Before I left intake, Josue approached me with a digital camera.

"We need this for head counts," he said.

I had cut my hair before I committed myself. I had thin eyebrows, which I overplucked, and I wanted bangs to cover them as they grew out. I was meticulous in my preparation. I packed books and lotion and shower gel and every outfit I felt I could wallow in: dark clothes and cotton tee shirts.

He took my picture, and I asked to see it.

"Another," I said.

He had forgotten how sure of myself I could sound. He took another, and told me I could have smiled. He escorted me up two floors to the women's ward. It was late, so the workers showed me to my room and gave me a paper cone of water and two pills—I don't know what. I had to change into a hospital gown so they could examine what I wore. They said they would give it back to me soon.

I am familiar with death, and I remembered it was heavy to hold. My mother's death was violent, internally. I remember once an elder skinned a rabbit in our yard. He wanted to teach me how to do it. He said so many times that a body is a universe. He slit the rabbit open and pointed with his knife to the thick parts of it. He said the word *entropy*. I remembered that when my mother died, a tube had stretched open the dry corners of her mouth. She was not given grace into the next world. When they pulled the tube from her throat, her lips were dry, and her mouth fell open.

Nothing is too ugly for this world, I think. It's just that people pretend not to see.

I fell asleep trying to remember the composition of

a tooth. Gum and bone support the softer things. The raw nerve in my tooth tingled under the weight of my tongue. I don't want my mouth to be obscene when I die.

I was finally beneath myself at a new low.

In the morning, I was the only one dressed in my hospital gown for breakfast. The nurses walked me back to my room and explained I should wear my clothes, which were put away in my dresser.

I asked the women if there was a scale to weigh myself. I weighed a hundred and twenty-two pounds the day before. They pointed to my dresser and left the room. There's no right way to dress in the hospital. Some women were dressed provocatively. I put on my cotton shirt and leggings, thinking of what threads weighed the least.

In line, a stringy-blond woman who looked ill talked about meth, and everything she said seemed like a small lie. I stood behind her and just let her lead the way. Her feet and mouth seemed so urgent and dangerous.

The cafeteria was coed, and the men looked violent. I didn't eat because I considered the pills I had taken might have been the type that made me hungry—the type that allowed me to eat until I'd realize I was full. It feels like a skill to refrain. The benefit in this place is that I must refrain from you. I can't physically see you or know what you're doing.

The nurses escorted us back to the ward, and then they pulled me aside for a full tour. The brunette nurse asked me if I believed in God, and the smart one said I looked heartbroken.

"Is this about a man?" she said.

I felt breathless, like every question was a step up a stairway.

Casey, it was more than surreal. I needed a drink, but I reminded myself not to say that out loud, even in jest. The women walked me to the reading room.

"Nobody reads in here," the smart one said. "It's quiet."

The nurses smelled good because everything in there, including us, was sterilized and without distinction. They smelled like their homes and lunches and living.

"You're welcome to read so long as it doesn't take away from your healing," the brunette said. "We have romance novels in stock and some books from the Oprah Book Club."

I did enjoy Oprah.

The art room was all colored paper, glue, and glitter. The pool was stagnant. The birds outside offended me—domestic but free. All the rooms were stark white, but the lighting was dim so everyone looked bleaker. A dull blue stripe ran along every room for the invalids to follow. They gave me an Ambien, and I walked the line, stopping at every barred window. I wanted to hear the world, but the glass was too thick.

It was funny and hurtful to see the women walking past my room to glimpse at me and assess what type of crazy I was. Every few minutes I saw a new girl who looked sad or angry. We mirrored each other's blank stares. It was nice to feel at home in that odd place. I tidied my room like I never do at home.

You said you love to failure. I made you full and flushed. You loved me until your body failed your will. You said making love was kissing my eyelids. I kept them open once and saw you differently. You rooted against me and forced my eyes closed like little coffins. I wondered how many bitter ghosts it took to create a cold feeling in a room. My face was covered in your sweat. I was all points and sharp corners before I loved you.

You don't appreciate that you've broken me. Lovers want to undo their partners. I feel unveiled and more work than you had bargained for. I was unsure of the currency of men and unaware that losing myself would feel so physical.

I remember when I spent the night with you once: In the morning I wanted to order a proper breakfast with potatoes and an egg, with toast, and another breakfast of French toast and maple syrup, and butter. You tell me it's too much. You don't think I'm gracious. I ordered the proper breakfast, and the server didn't bring me toast. I complained, and then she brought cold toast, and then I complained again, and then my food went cold. My eyes welled, and you looked disgusted. I usually don't care about that look. What right does a man have to look at me like that? I think it's justifiable to hurt someone when they look at me like that.

We fought for hours, and I didn't say that my mother had spent her life waiting for service. I waited with her in cafés for an order of french fries or something small we could afford. White women didn't greet her or consider our time. We walked into places and sometimes men heckled me. I said I was twelve, and they often didn't believe me. My mother and I found solace, driving hours out of our neighborhood, where being Indian was not much of a crime. If I told you that, I would also need to stop and note the significance of so many other things.

My mind is overwhelmed with breakfast alone. I don't eat for days so you can run your hands over my ribcage. You told me that you always want to eat ribs afterward. I don't eat for days because I can't afford it. The meal I order after being fucked, by you, or anyone, is something earned. Men objectify me, to such a degree that they forget I eat. You feed your dog more kindly than you feed me. That's men.

That was also my problem: an inability to distinguish you from other men when I am angry. I'm sorry. If only you could see how little I need in this hospital.

I have been vulnerable, but I have never felt this threatened before. I thought I knew what the worst outcomes could be, until I ended up here. I didn't know not being enough, or being so wrong about someone, would feel this way.

You got the message I asked my friend to relay. You left me a message, and the nurses said you sounded concerned. I called you from the community phone, but you were not available. I don't even know what to say, so I ask you to visit me. I hope that when you get my message you are alone. Nobody would advise you seeing me. You are capable of a finality I can't exact.

I sat in the reading room for five hours watching women color. The women in here take coloring seriously. They're territorial over the colors.

"That's an earthy green," Patricia said to me. "You should use something brighter."

Patricia looked bothered by my work. She was an apple-faced older woman, with white hair and a soft voice. She was taken here against her will, so she had no clothes of her own. Her breasts hung low in her gown.

"I don't know, Patricia," Laurie said. "It's kind of like a rich, lustery green. That's how green stems are."

Patricia smiled and passed me the right color.

Laurie told me that I should color and speak to the other women and never watch the TV because they write that stuff down. She doesn't want to be released because she is homeless. She tried to kill herself with pills, and by some magic, she was discovered on the floor in her own vomit. She was living in transitional housing, and the suicide attempt wasn't an issue, but when the emergency responders searched her room, they found pills, which had been prescribed, along with two beer cans. They had a strict rule about alcohol. She was notified with a little sticky note from the nurses that she could no longer live in her home, and that someone else would inhabit her studio by the time she got out.

"Tallboys?" I asked.

"No," she said. "It was two small cans."

Patricia hovered over her own flower to disengage from our talk.

"I didn't try anything," I said. "I usually do try something when I get this bad. I usually take pills and vomit or something."

Laurie's hair made me nostalgic for my childhood. It was auburn and permed and gelled into a crunchy lion's mane.

What I color is inside the lines and cute. A teacher's assistant in grade one asked me to draw a spoon. I took my time and drew an elaborate rainbow in its silhouette. I gave it a mouth and legs. She told me that passing relied on my ability to *just* draw a spoon, then she handed me another paper. I used to forgetfully bring things home from school to show my father, years after he left.

I have some memories of him painting. He held me tight in the cold of the basement. I used to sit on his lap for hours while he worked.

"Look," he said, pointing to one of his birds. "What do you see?"

"Eagle," I said.

"Mother," he said.

He looked a lot like Jim from *Taxi*. He had long, coarse hair, and he always wore light blue denim with an old baseball tee. He was lean, and my mother had a thing for tall, lean men.

I feel like I don't belong here, Casey. I feel like nothing here has helped. The psychiatrist advised against me leaving and threatened to get the courts involved. So I tried to engage myself with every material and exercise. They give each woman a large pink book that asks numerous questions to help parse out all the things that led up to their unraveling. The latter half of the book tries to wind the reader back together, asking them to find better ways to cope: Stop and think before you do something you regret. I don't like neat narratives or formulas.

I go to group therapy. It is quite intense, because holy shit there are a lot of women in the group who can articulate why they are here.

"It's been forty years of silence for me," said Laurie. "My father raped me from age six to ten."

The group counselor said that one must forgive for one's self and not for the perpetrator. This made little-to-no sense in my mind. We're all on meds here, most of us are half zombie and half antsy: a weird mix. In white culture, forgiveness is synonymous with letting go. In my culture, I believe we carry pain until we can reconcile with it through ceremony. Pain is not framed like a problem with a solution. I don't even know that white people see transcendence the way we do. I'm not sure that their dichotomies apply to me.

I found myself staring off during group, which made the counselor, Terri, prompt me for my story.

"I look for external validations of worth, and I always end up crazy over it," I said.

"It's good you can acknowledge that," Terri said. "How long have you been doing that?"

"My whole life. Isn't that what we learn as children? To look for affirmation in the external? Our fathers and mothers?" I said.

"Some children are taught self-esteem from a young age," she said.

"Oh," I said.

There's a girl with tight braids who posts up against the wall at group therapy. When Terri asks her to sit down, she says she doesn't want to. She says that she has to be here for seven full days, no matter if she behaves or not.

Terri explained self-esteem and its function, and I blame my mother for not saying these things. My mother wasn't big on esteem for herself, let alone trying to foster that in me. I think self-esteem is a white invention to further separate one person from another. It asks people to assess their values and implies people have worth. It seems like identity capitalism.

Mom did teach me story, though, along with Grampa Crow. She knew that was my power, and she knew women need their power honed early, before it's beaten out of them by the world. I know what you're thinking, Casey, *again* with my mother? Yes, unfortunately that's the biggest part of my work in this place. The therapists seem to think she's a link to my betterment. I think she did the best she could with the tools she had. The therapist said that's making excuses. Sometimes she had to lock herself away from the world, that's all. I have fond and bitter memories of her. I can't imagine what she'd think of me being here. My mother would have laughed at me. She'd have rolled in laughter and thrown her head back at my misery.

She believed in subversion and turning things upside down. She mocked everything. My desire to be normal or sincere made her laugh.

"Men will never love you," she said once. "They'll use you up, and, when you're bone dry and it's your time to write, you'll be alone without a goddamn typewriter to your name."

She had a lot taken from her. False starts took something out of her, and then having children and getting married, and then divorced. All the jobs she had—and then there was the work at her desk, and the several books she wrote.

I feel like my body is being drawn through a syringe. Sometimes walking is hard. The gravity of Indian women's situations, and the weight of our bodies, are too much.

Even Mom's cynicism was subversive. She often said nothing would work out. She often said that trying was futile and still dedicated her life to other people through social work. When she was unemployed, she rallied for social justice. She did things that required hopefulness. She made a name as an angry Indian woman who could consent and disallow things. Indian women are usually discouraged from that basic agency. Not to say that she wasn't betrayed and hurt.

I remember well that I had to take care of myself. When I was a child, and I was as restless as I am now, I walked along the walls of our home, waiting for someone to come home and feed me or bathe me or take me outside. The phone rang once, and it was the unemployment office. I told the woman that my mother was at work. I thought lies were good when they made someone seem good. The strange thing about poverty is that maintaining a level of desperation and lack of integrity keeps the checks rolling in.

Days after I picked up the phone, my mother lost her unemployment. She screamed until she cried, and then said that if we didn't eat it was my fault. I know, just like I know with my own child, she was sorry the moment the words escaped her mouth. The difference between her and I, as mothers, is that I don't have a sense of pride with my son. He is a small king. Still, he is as unfortunate as me, but at least he hasn't had to be home alone or starve. I have fostered love with compliments and carrying him, even when he grew to be half my size. I prepared meals and spoon-fed him. Children are teachers.

My mother's burning ceremony was irreverent like her. We had plates of smoked salmon and the things our grandparents liked to eat, ready for the fire to take, and I heard someone joke they would put some wine in for Karen. The fire exploded across the lawn, and people said that it was Mom. It was that night I felt compelled to resist all the traditionalism of my mother, because I'm not sure how it served her children.

She hated alcohol and stopped drinking before I was born. She was a pipe carrier and fasted alone in the mountains anytime she had to. She built a sweat lodge by herself. She taught my brothers how to keep a fire and taught me how to prepare a feast. She spent years of my life waking up with the day to give thanks to the river.

I never understood her commitment to living well. It seems innate that I am fucked up. I think I have the blood memory of my neurotic ancestors and their vices. Her work seems as important as my work, to acknowledge that some of my people slept in, and wasted their lives, and were gluttonous.

For her burial, my brothers and I walked her ashes in a cedar box from the church to the grave. Dogs lingered behind the party. My aunt says at every funeral, there are some cultures where women are paid to wail—are revered for wailing better than others. There is a culture that makes crying a virtue and a gift.

It felt like Mom's funeral lasted a year. It felt like one long winter, where my family told every story of hers by memory, as if we were being interrogated. My mother's spirit loomed over us, imploring us to avenge her death, but there were too many culprits: from the government, to the reservation, to her own family, to whoever hurt her the very first time. I saw in pictures that between thirteen and fourteen my mother changed. That culprit, and then all our fathers, and the men who said they were down for the cause and then abandoned it, like they did their children—those men killed my mother. Even the sweet lovers who gave her hope are the culprits of her pain.

It's strange that my grandmother and my mother

and my aunts died from blood clots or cancer. I think again of entropy and of the body.

When my mother had her first aneurism, I received a call from my siblings. I swear two of them held the receiver. They said, maybe in unison, "Mom misses you. She isn't speaking."

I don't like to say I am the sensible one in my family, because we all are dependent on each other. Maybe I am the logical mechanism in the family, and I shudder to think that, with me here in a crazy house. They told me she was walking into walls. I called emergency and booked a flight home.

I ran away from her as a girl, and a blood clot called me back.

The first thing she did when she saw me was laugh. She didn't have the capacity to speak. They said she hadn't made any noises until I arrived.

I touched her foot first and started a routine of questions to make her happy: Is there cable here? My show is on. I don't trust the white women with the IV—they'll do you like they do in the soaps. We're going to need a sign language for all the insults you can't call us. How will we know when you want to hit us?

She was so small that her snarling was endearing. I always made her laugh.

What little I have told you in the past seemed problematic. You seemed engaged by my dysfunction because you are a writer and not because I had experienced it. It is odd that I went to foster care while my mother worked in a group home. But it was not odd to me.

I can only elaborate on the small things, like her smallness, and how light her fists were—how she pinched the fat of my fingers to tell me she loved me. She was always aware of her struggle. A single mother with four children is destined to die from exhaustion, unless there is a miracle of fortune or justice.

We came close to fortune and justice when I was a kid. Paul Simon needed correspondence that my mother had written long before to a man named Salvador Argón, the subject of a Broadway play he was writing. Sal was sentenced to death row at age sixteen for murdering two other teenagers. He earned a degree on the inside and became an activist. That's how he met Mom.

She spoke about Sal like I speak about you. We should have wanted for simpler things, but in many ways my mother taught me love was divine—like a hermitage or vision or picking from the tree of knowledge. Mother didn't like the Bible, but I appreciate it for how suffering is related to profundity.

Paul Simon called while I was watching TV. Our landline was screwed into the old seventies wood panel of our kitchen wall. I was ashamed of the house. The room was barren. There was an orange, thrift shop dinette set, and a shrine on our counter for Stevie Ray Vaughan. It was a picture of him surrounded by barks and sage my mother picked, with red ties and turquoise jewelry. The bracelets and rings were gifts from my uncle Lyle, a jeweler who idolizes Elvis and wore a bouffant until old age turned it into a less voluminous side part.

Mom was in the bath. Paul's voice was timid. He asked for Mom. I yelled to her that Paul was on the line. Mom told me to keep him on the phone while I heard her body emerge—splashes and her small wet feet running.

"How old are you?" Simon asked.

"I'm ten. What do you do?" I asked.

"I'm an artist," he said.

I told him that was nice and asked him what kind of art. He laughed at me.

My mother, wrapped in a towel, ripped the phone from my hand. She carried on several conversations like this. I began to suspect they were flirting when I went with Mom to the library to look up if Simon had a wife. I didn't want Paul Simon to be my new father. I saw an album cover once. He wore turtlenecks. He was pasty. He had beady eyes.

"He's married to some redhead, I think. White woman," Mom said. We had seen some news clippings and rented a biography. He was a god, and not the personalized one of benevolence, but the type who could take things away.

She sent him every letter between herself and Salvador Agrón. I had read the letters in our basement. There were images of horses and dirt and bodies, and nothing of love until it became all about love. Simon was inspired by Salvador's plight.

Mother's narrative was eventually drowned in Simon's version of it all, and nowhere was Sal's story. He was dead.

We became self-important Indians with every call. Mom floated around the house after three-day shifts at a group home and became happy. After years of writing manically in her room, someone was finally using her words. A camera crew came to interview Mom. I recently saw film of her, where a narrator with a rich English accent said, "Paul Simon and his team researched every detail of the story. They even located Wahzinak. She offered Paul Simon her intimate memories of Sal's character."

"He was much more beautiful in real life," my mother said. "He just illuminated. His prose was phenomenal. He could talk about the prison life. He could talk about his poverty. People come along and they grace your life, and they make it extraordinary."

After the interview my mother cried into the phone, and she didn't speak to us. She didn't sit at the table; she sat on the floor. I watched her body shake. Maybe it was having cameras in our rotting home. It was infested with mold and ladybugs and old furniture we didn't wear down ourselves. Maybe that's my shame talking. Maybe it was that Indians are at a ripe age when they're fifty, and Mother was there. Maybe it was that Salvador was kind.

She met a serpent in prison who was my father. The same provocation and sentimentality drew her in, and he wasn't kind. The legend is that he was banished from the house after many transgressions, and that we all waited by the door with weapons in case he came back, even me, a baby then, holding a hammer or a bat or a broom or a doll. The story has shifted because it's not funny anymore.

Simon gave us a choice: American dollars or a family trip to New York. Julia Roberts attended the opening. A woman who would later star in *Grey's Anatomy* played my mom. We missed the opportunity to see it all to buy school clothes. Mom spent the rest on bills, food, and things.

It could have redeemed her, like my words on the page—like I would have myself believe articulating her grace and pain could be redemptive. I didn't want Paul Simon to be my father, but I wanted him to save us. More than a few thousand—I wanted him to see us and decide we were worth a play in our own right. I wanted him to see my mother, beyond a groupie, or a cliché, or an Indian woman—because she was more. He didn't see her.

The play reduced Mom to an "Indian hippie chick," as *Variety*'s Greg Evans called her. A "prison groupie," and I had only known her as an outreach worker. Prison was part of that, getting them to write or draw, to find sanity in isolation. I'm trying not to make excuses, because she did fall. It's in the text and on my mind every day how she fell. It could be like Eve. The old texts say we get menses for the fall, feel pain for the fall. God couldn't watch it; he sent us his boy, but I doubt he watched his son die. I think he just waited for him on the other side.

One of my mother's old friends, Richard, wrote about her breasts and Salvador's womanizing for his non-fiction book. He wrote with provocation and sentimentality while the iron was hot. Dick flew from California to Seabird to show Mom the book. He told me about his Jeep and that he would take me to the city someday, and Mom grew suspicious. He handed her the book after tea. She went to her room, came out, and told him to leave. Mother cried. I found the book underneath her bed and understood the contents like Hildegard, a prophet without an education. Her heart was inflamed, and she knew the scriptures and the gospel. She didn't understand the tenses or the division of syllables, but she could read it.

The pain was a process to understanding. Men were born to hurt my mother in the flesh and the text, and she was my savior. The language was always wrong. Even in this account I can't convey the pulse of her. In her sleep I couldn't turn away, in love with her heavy breathing. She rarely slept, but, when she did, it felt generative and sacred like a bear's hibernation. Her small palms were red with heat. She always fell asleep with a book on her chest. It was the illumination of living light.

You were my only visitor this week. I'm surprised you came. I said nothing I meant to say. You said ambiguous things: Maybe in the future . . . You want the best for me.

You are going to Colorado for Christmas. You brought a bra for Patricia like I asked.

Patricia cried when I gave it to her. Her family lives away from her, and when her husband died, she wanted to die. She seemed certain that it was her time. Sometimes suicidality doesn't seem dark; it seems fair.

The therapist says that instead of thinking of the loss of you, I must visualize a space for myself and focus on the details of that space. I have old spaces in my registry to recall. I think of you often, but there are still spaces unchanged by you.

Uncle Harold's shack: a teal, crisp marshmallow since his wife allegedly burned it down, with him in it. I can imagine the charred teddy bear in the middle of his den. I run my hands over the craggy ends of every black cupboard. I wonder what Uncle Harold looks like in his grave. His hair is twelve dead strands that stick to my hand. His knuckles look like Liberace's, because, thank god, my mother and her siblings were flamboyant. He has long, white cuffs. His slacks are wool and pleated. His brown mouth is closed and tight. I've gone mentally to Uncle's home, and his grave, because of the intrusive thought that while I color in the evenings you are sitting across from a woman at a restaurant table. While I'm walking along dull-blue lines or gluing Popsicle sticks, you are with a white woman named Laura. She plays tennis. She's an ethereal white woman who thinks dogs are people too. You think, *Isn't this nice*. You're tempted to mention the sad woman in the hospital, your ex. It might assuage your guilt or get you laid, and it might kill me to imagine this here.

You tell her that your last relationship was all-consuming.

When you told me that I want too much, I considered how much you take.

Laura tells you that she got out of something too. She has a frailty I don't have. Even if I never ate again, I could not present myself so meekly: bird-boned Laura. You treat her like a pal and are happy with the passionless art of settling—of forgetting.

I try not to imagine you laughing at her dog stories.

I return to Harold's home. It's dark. Abandoned. It's night. The old, dead walls are illuminated by the truck stop across the street. I can hear you telling me that the shack will fall on me. By the time I get out of this hospital you'll be missing the smell of her on your pillow.

I tried to cry into a wall as silently as I could. I tried to call my friend to get me from your house. It would be dangerous to forgive you for that kind of abandonment. I think it's dangerous to let go of a transgression when the transgressor is not contrite. I think of myself in black lingerie, crying against your adobe wall.

It might hurt you to know that another man loves me, but I'm not sure. For several days I did crazy things before I committed myself. I begged you to see me. I went to your bar, and my friends let me have my grief, in long drives, close to your home, while they explained that love is like this. They read endless letters of mine and told me that it was all enough. I was enough and sometimes people break up. I felt juvenile. A friend is in love with me, and when the town lit the luminaries outside of your bar on a December night, I told him that I was not finished loving you.

At the bar, he and I sat next to each other. I felt like a child—I was too short on the stool, resting both hands on my coaster. I told him that none of his caring made me feel better. He knows you're not my only problem. My relationship with you felt integral. Many things were infinitesimal. Combined, there's a whole thing I can't bear. I needed you. I told him that I turned you off so many times, and he refused to believe I was the problem.

"You cried." He shrugs his shoulders. "He could have let you be fucking crazy, and then just brought you a beer."

I start to cry and he says no repeatedly and quickly. He has ADHD, and since I'm manic, we're aligned in reaction. He takes my hands from my face and puts them on the coaster.

"Indian women die early," I say. "I think this up and down . . . and it's not the first time I've centered myself in the love of a man . . . My son doesn't need to witness this. I should have been spared from the life my mother gave to me."

"Statistically, white men are more likely to kill themselves. If you're going to go, it will probably be something else. Don't die. Casey's an asshole. You're not perfect—but this type of fucked-up you got, it's not that bad, Terese."

He consoled me in letters and visits with books. Before I came to the hospital, he stopped me outside of an editorial meeting. He told me to be strong. He put a letter and a book, *Just Kids*, in my hands.

I don't think that I am lonely. I think that I am starved and maybe ravenous for the very thing you withhold from me.

The first chapter in your book is titled "Wanting/Not-Having." You and I had a joke between us that I want you back, time and again, because I prefer wanting. Even when I am there with you, beneath your breath, I still feel you withholding. It's like your breath—that I know you've never had a cavity. You lean back and open your mouth. Your mouth is so large and unashamed. I feel jealous and amorous when you tell me that.

I am partly sorry for the night I cried in front of you and began to hit myself. You had never seen me do that before. Before, I was just temperamental about breakfast. The therapists reiterate that when I'm suicidal nobody is beholden to me. You have the right to walk away. I don't understand, though, why you would look at me the way you did.

They have given me brochures about being the child of a narcissistic mother. That's laughable. They tell me I don't fit the criteria of histrionic, but I thought I did after speaking to some of the other women who were diagnosed like that. I fit the criteria of an adult child of an alcoholic and the victim of sexual abuse. I reiterate to the therapists several stories about my eldest brother's abuse and my sister's. I often have felt, in proximity to their violations, that I mimic their chaos.

They moved my release, and they want me to stay the full seven days, which means I'll miss Christmas Eve with my son. I wish I could exchange my time with Laurie. She's being released today. She told me that if she had insurance they would have kept her in the hospital, and that they're keeping me longer because I have good insurance. I can't say she's wrong because an insurance representative works with my psychiatrist concerning my release and my progress.

I'm upset to stay here longer than I expected. But I think I like these walls. It feels artificial but good. The psychiatrist likes to speak to me more than she does the other women. She calls me in, and sometimes our discussions become more general and conversational. She wants to know whether I've considered contacting you after this. I told her that I don't believe you're a hindrance, and that I am not prideful in love.

"He isn't telling me to leave him alone," I said.

"You're an intelligent and attractive woman. I doubt that this is easy for either of you," she said.

"I think I could leave him alone."

She gives me the full report of my conditions. I have Posttraumatic Stress Disorder, and an eating disorder, and I have bipolar II.

"When you get out I hope you have a good Christmas," she said.

The girl with the tight braids, Jackie, keeps looking at me and saying that something isn't right. I ask her if I have crazy eyes, and she says no. She talks to me all day and French braids my hair. She likes to drink, and she doesn't know why I can't just find another man. "I guess it is that easy," I say. "If I wasn't sentimental." She only dates thugs, she says. She runs down the ways she meets men, and it sounds exhausting.

Jackie encourages me to eat, and the things I've eaten today were reasonable. There was rice pilaf and broccoli, and I still drank the prune juice the cafeteria workers put aside for me.

I weigh a hundred and twenty-six pounds now. It is progress that I know my weight is not the issue. Still, I've obsessively weighed myself, and it's inconvenient for the nurses, because they have to escort me to and from the gym before meals.

On Christmas, I wake up at four in the morning. The nurses let me sit by a window, and I look out at the highway and imagine that the people driving to work are good. I feel like I could master containment that way.

Josue came from behind me and tapped me with an envelope.

"You're getting out today," he said.

"Santa," I said.

"Can I give you a hug?" he asked.

He hugged me until the tension in my back relaxed. His Christmas card simply said that I had talent, and that part of what makes me a good person is that I can be struck by emotion. He also included the picture of me he took.

I've been released, but I am not better. I can't work, and I won't leave the house. Outpatient treatment: Because I am not crazy enough to be sedated in a madhouse. They think I'm better. I am a cat in heat— something my mother would say. I am unraveling in the dark kitchen. I am scattering my wet eyes looking for signs or something significant. I am incorrigible when I'm like this. I wish I could do anything but stand alone in a dark kitchen without you.

Every Christmas after Grandmother died, my mother locked herself in her room to cry. We always stood on the other side of her door, looking at each other as if she might never stop crying. Some years she didn't come out until the morning. Some years she came out with red eyes, and she could barely speak. She'd motion to get the presents from under the tree. We passed them around, and I can't remember a single present I ever received.

I lock myself away as she does. Some things seem too perfectly awful.

I only have crude things to say to you. I won't fuck

you anymore so it can mean less. I might be gone, but you can still see me with a black light in your mattress. There is permanence in physical craft. Laura isn't absorbed in any beds. She barely perspires. She requires twenty-four-hour protection from her own scent. She keeps her bra on. She wears practical clothes. Her fleeces and cargo pants and that smell of non-scented goat's milk lotion for dry skin—that must do something for you.

My body left resonance that can't be dismantled or erased. I don't know if men think about what seduction is. It was reading the work you love, and buying clothes, and making polite conversation with your friends—convincing your mother that I could mother you like she does. It was laying warm towels across my legs before I shaved so that when you touched me, I was soft. It was withholding from you at the right times, and listening to you with my eyes and ears. I worked hard to assert intent on your bed and your body. I've soiled all beds for you with my wanting and preparation. I prepared myself for you as if I wasn't working as a server, going to college, or raising Isaiah. The weight and the dust of me are in every thread of your mattress. Love is tactile learning, always, first and foremost.

When you loved me it was degrading. Using me for love degraded me worse. You should have just fucked me. It was degenerative. You inside me, outside, then I leave, then I come back, get fucked, you look down at me and say, "I love you. I love you." I go home and degenerate alone. The distinctness of my bed and its corners are fucked by my fucking you. My agency is degraded. For comfort, I remember my hospital bed and the neutrality of the room I had. I was safe from myself and from you. I'm stupid, waiting for the phone to ring, thinking you might call. I'd drive to you and be no better for it.

I want my grandmother's eyes on me. I thought un-seeing would be a cruel game to play with myself. But now I am reading the dark and knowing how my feet drag on every inch—feeling monstrous and tired. I'd like to have familiarity back, but all I see now is my fa-ther's body over my mother, whose body is boneless like a rabbit's. I've descended into my earliest memory. It is too horrible to know, and no work of unseeing will re-move him from me, or turn the lights on in the kitchen. How could someone like you ever be on the other side of the door—on the other side of this?

4

IN A PECAN FIELD

I wrote like I had something to prove to you. The stories were about the Indian condition alongside the mundane. Most of the work felt like a callback to traditional storytelling. Salish stories are a lot like its art: sparse and interested in blank space. The work must be striking.

It was spring, and I hadn't stopped wanting you. I sent you letters. I bought a tripod to take pictures of my body and my loneliness.

I told my therapist that I felt no purpose without you.

"What about your children?" she asked.

"I believe purpose extends beyond family."

"It's been months, and he hasn't reached out. Do you think we're at an impasse?"

Leaving her office, I thought most people would have walked away with the realization that it was over.

With the knowledge of what a normal person might do, I tried to enact it all. I went wherever I was invited and invested in my friendships. My son and I had long discussions about family and what he might want in the future.

"I think Casey would be a good dad," he said.

"Yeah," I said.

"Remember that guy who got me a PlayStation?" he asked.

"Chris."

"Why isn't he your friend anymore?"

"He was my boyfriend, Isaiah." He looked shocked. We laughed. He has given me so much laughter. "I would not be able to live without you."

"I know," he said.

Isaiah has always known his brother. We made frequent visits. Because I was Canadian and a flight risk, I had supervised visitation only.

I remember one visit at the YWCA. Isadore was three, and he hadn't yet learned how to sit properly or hold a conversation. I gave him a grin and tickled his tummy. He crawled underneath the desk and I followed. There was so much laughter, and then the supervisor asked us to be quiet. Isadore sat in his chair and rubbed his eyes.

"Do you need something?" I asked.

"Grandma," he said.

I held him, and we cut our visit short an hour. The supervisor wrote a lot in her notebook. She shook her head at me. I asked her what was wrong.

"It's not a good sign you don't want to spend the full two hours with your child."

"I did," I said. It was all I could say.

Visits went like that, and I didn't want to put Isaiah through it. I let Isaiah go with my ex-husband and his family to spend time with each other as often as I could bear. Vito never asked to visit, and I wondered why, never out loud.

Through all of this, I believe Isaiah learned that I needed him. Things were so complicated. I think he felt compelled to need me more than most children need their mothers.

With my son in mind, I decided to date men who I couldn't see a future with—men who would never meet him. He had been exposed to so much with his brother and his father. I couldn't just move forward in life with another man, but I didn't want to be lonely.

Eric looked at me a lot on our dates. It was a focused stare that made me forget the abandonment I felt. We had an English class together a long time ago, and he had gone away to study abroad in London and then to L.A.

The first time Eric and I sat down together he asked me what I wanted to drink, and I asked for a Michelob ULTRA. He scoffed and said he hadn't ordered one of those in years. I didn't leave then—it was an indication as to my state.

I asked him polite things: what is it like to be back? Will you go to grad school? Can I taste your beer?

"You're ethnically ambiguous, and I feel like you should be capitalizing on it," he said.

"Oh no . . ."

"I'm sorry," he said.

"Are you an ethnic enthusiast?" I asked.

"What?"

We asked questions we shouldn't have. I revealed I was still in love with my ex. He told me that his ex couldn't deal with his bipolar cycles.

"The pendulum swings—like a motherfucker," he said.

I told him I was bipolar, and he already knew.

"I walked into traffic, and then I was taken to the hospital. I decided that when I got out I'd move somewhere there was less shit to do—focus on me," he said.

"I was in the hospital. I'm not really sure I'm better," I said.

"The pendulum."

We went to his place and drank beer and watched stand-up until he asked me what we were doing. He held his face with long fingers—I peeled them one by one until he opened his eyes.

"Nothing," I said.

With someone to talk to, I started to enjoy myself. He introduced me to his friends, and purposefully said I was brilliant. He barely touched me or told me I was pretty. He weighed less than I did. He didn't mind anything about me. He was enamored with the convenience—we were both ill and alone and intelligent.

I remembered what it was to be desired, if only for

my mind. There was a man just before Casey, who had arranged fireworks on our first date, "in case it didn't happen on its own." It felt obligatory to kiss him—to reject him soon after. And Casey, in his boxers, once answered the door to a fruit basket the man sent me, asking for another shot. I watched Casey's large mouth, full of pineapple, smirking at me—almost angry. Another man, he came to my door with cookies, and one man sent me a puzzle I didn't put together, with some latitude and longitude for a restaurant he wanted to take me to, all while Casey was there, witnessing, and maybe it was seeing this that made him so resistant to me—to wanting or needing.

Eric's arms were never heavy when he held me in bed. He felt like a thin blanket. He held me before I left in the morning and told me we could make pancakes. We could do anything, if I had time. He was unafraid of me, in the daylight, at any time—I felt enough.

Eric and I occasionally cried or sent each other long tangents about things we were only momentarily inspired by. It was good to be given every benefit of every doubt. I had composed two packages of work and applied for an M.F.A. program at our college and at the Institute of American Indian Arts. The latter was a long shot. The flyer had pictures of famous Native authors on it—it was low residency and expensive. Some professors at our college had never found my work sophisticated enough. I lacked form and technique.

I emailed you that I was applying for an M.F.A. You responded with an exclamation mark or some well-wish.

I enjoyed the M.A. at our college. I went to class every

Tuesday and Thursday, and sometimes we'd be cross-ing the parking lot at the same time. Sometimes you hugged me.

A professor told me that I was to be accepted into both programs, and he was close to both institutions. He told me that whoever offers me the most money should be my choice. He promised that he would spread the rumor around that the university needed a writer like me.

A few days later, a professor asked me to stop by his office to talk about the program and my potential.

"You are a champ, Terese," he said.

"Thank you."

"You've taken feedback and come back harder. You're just an outstanding student."

"Thank you."

I had never felt sophisticated enough at the institu-tion, and in my creative writing classes, I only felt like I was seen as the graduate student Casey had been with.

"Have you seen Casey around?" he asked.

"Yes. He could be more miserable if you ask me."

He smiled.

"Our breakup was hard for me," I said.

"I've seen you around with a new guy," he offered.

There were multiple guys. I had made a point of spending time with a few of the writers on campus be-cause they provided free editing and feedback.

"I'm just rebounding."

"Casey was always a serious person. He's sad. It would be unpleasant to be around, I suppose?"

"I think I was the difficult one," I said.

"He said you wanted too much."

I don't remember following up with a question or if I used those moments to sell myself as an M.F.A. candidate. I just wanted to leave.

I drove straight to your house. I was angry. I knew that I wasn't *too much*. A man had shown me that *too much* could be managed through kindness and recognition.

You opened the door with a goofy smile. Before I said anything you asked me to come in for a beer.

I sat at your kitchen table, and you spoke to me while you put a pizza in the oven, and you cut cookie dough. Your house was clean for a writing man's home. You had new furnishings, which, no doubt, your mother bought you. Still, I cared what you thought about me.

"I make pecan sandies now," you said.

You looked content. You moved with certainty and were familiar with your kitchen—cooking was your new hobby.

"Is this what you do to get over me?" I asked.

"Yes."

You fed me and were forthcoming about adjusting to being single and missing my son. We sat across from each other. I let you tell me about other women. Time had passed, not long, but enough.

"She's just nice," you said.

"Yeah?"

"She puts the toilet seat up when she's done peeing." You seemed like you were bragging.

"Who the fuck would do that?" I said.

"Are you going to stay at the university here?"

"I don't know. I'm working on a Preparing Future Faculty application to see if they'll pay me to do my work here."

"With Lily?"

"Yeah."

Lily was my academic adviser, and she was priming me to be under her instruction. She had sent me her syllabus for a class in speculative fiction, and she wanted me to eventually work for the university.

"I was just out with her," you said.

"Oh?"

"She was a little drunk and asked if I wanted to cuddle."

"Wow."

You laughed. "You'd be happy to know," you said.

"What?" I asked.

"None of these women hold a candle to you."

You drank your beer and smirked.

"I still want you," I said.

You didn't look shocked, but you looked concerned. You put your hand across the table, and I put mine on top of yours. We were both impressed with how comforting it felt to touch each other.

"Mountain Woman," you said. My Indian name.

I let go and stood up. Not to threaten that I might leave, but I wanted you to see me. "I'm regulated now," I said.

You approached me, and we made love on your counter. My tailbone bruised. Passion seemed so endless when we were in it. It seemed like, in those moments, we could have pushed each other into anything—into saying anything.

I told you that I loved you numerous times, and you reciprocated. I had forgotten the man you were before you saw me out of control. You had loved me like a man with the capacity to keep his promises and sacrifice for his family. You loved me completely, with a type of trust I didn't realize was rare.

You were so different from Eric's aimlessness. You were so different from the men who have cowered from me. You were different from the men who made a challenge out of hurting me.

We had full hearts for each other, still. While you were sleeping, I considered that I might tell you it was my entire fault. How could it be yours? When you're like this?

We got up for class. Before I left I hugged you. I looked up and asked if we could be a family. You said that we couldn't be a family, and you didn't look at me when you said it. You told me you loved me. We both started crying. I thought you were being careful with me. I thought that you were guarding yourself—what pride you had left was worth a lot. You had a human being who put the toilet seat up for you. You had a person who wasn't "all consuming," like a black hole.

I went back. I went back more than once or four times or five. Every time, you were baking, or enjoying your quiet life alone. Once, you had a woman there. I still went back, later. You let me in every time. Eventually, I stopped asking if we could be together again.

♥

Eric became less appealing, but we became more comfortable with each other.

"You don't need to make noises," he said, on top of me.

"What?"

"I just don't want you to perform sex for me."

And yet I did. He wrapped me in a *Star Wars* blanket and stared at the ceiling. We were both manic and unable to sleep.

"Do you want to drink?" he said.

He talked about his ex-girlfriend, and he said that he felt like he was going to have a breakdown. I talked about you, and he said that I wouldn't ever be sane enough. He said that there was nothing I could do to convince you that I was not crazy, and why would I want to?

He asked me about the future.

That was our last night together, because it was enough. I realized that love can be mediocre and a safe comfort, or it can be unhinged and hurtful. Either seemed like a good life.

My therapist wasn't disappointed in me. She congratulated me for analyzing my situation with you and considering how I was accountable for your mistrust.

"I am worried, though," she said.

"I'm not going to break down again."

"Not that. I'm worried that he's using you."

"It's much deeper than sex. He tells me that he loves me and explains carefully why he can't be with me. He considers me."

"You're in a vulnerable position. Months ago, you were in the hospital with suicidal ideation. He should consider how telling you that he loves you could make you feel. He should consider how having sex with you, and then explaining why he can't be with you, is manipulative."

I defended you. I knew that you did love me and telling me about other women *was* hurtful, but I stayed with you those nights on my own regard. If you were hurting me, I knew it was not intentional.

"I'll give him a timeline. After three months I will begin to see other people seriously."

My therapist was impressed with my solution and worried that I was giving you three more months than you needed.

The Institute of American Indian Arts offered me a scholarship. I accepted. The program was designed with a renaissance in mind. When people were trying to conceptualize a program for Native writers, they said it would be a renaissance.

I met with Lily briefly just to see the status of our efforts, to see if our college would compete with IAIA. I sat with her at a café. She was in the middle of a stack of papers. She was sweet. I told her, because I had nothing to lose, that I had been wearing the same shirt for three days. I was busy with my son and writing and the last of my classes.

She told me to look at what she was wearing: floral shorts and a mustard brown shirt. She shrugged her shoulders, and we laughed. She began to tell me about a man she was seeing, long distance, and that he was brilliant, and she was a mess.

"I'm still a mess with Casey."

"I didn't know you were still seeing him," she said.

"I came here from his house."

"Casey is so cool."

"I believe you're my mentor. I want to say that you knew Casey and I had broken up recently, and asking him if he wanted to cuddle isn't okay with me."

"Oh, god! No! I have very different relationships with my friends. This is a misunderstanding."

"I just don't want to talk to you about this."

"When you guys broke up he was heartbroken."

"Did he talk about me?"

"Not much."

She started to talk about other writers we knew and who was incompetent and who was going to do nothing with their M.F.A.s. I drank piñon coffee and laughed at her jokes.

"I just want to say—I don't know why Casey would have told you about me asking him that. Why do you think he told you?"

"He's stupid. He's always been thoughtless."

She consoled me about you. She says that you love me. She wants to believe that you love me, I can tell. Romantics can be comforting.

You started to hold me more, and when I brought Isaiah to your home, you both rejoiced.

You made him his favorite meal: macaroni and cheese. You invited Lily over and she sat next to my son and complimented his manners. I was nobody to tell you who you could ask to your house. Isaiah had just got a haircut, and I dressed him up to see you. We all sat at the table, and then my son got quiet.

"What, baby?" I asked.

"Just," Isaiah said.

"Are you hungry?" I asked.

Lily excused herself from the table to smoke outside.

You observed my son and I, and by your face, I knew you didn't know to be concerned for my son when he sunk down the way he did.

"There's crumbs on it," Isaiah said.

The macaroni had breadcrumbs on the top of it.

"Be polite," I said.

He sinks deeper into his chair and won't look at me. He regressed, and he was predictably easy to fix, but I didn't want him to act this way in front of you.

You went outside to join Lily. I was more worried about how you might change your mind on us than I was worried about my son's heart. And when I recognized that, I knew you weren't ready for us. My baby was still dependent on me. He was even dependent on me to show him he could love you again.

I walked up to him and crouched down to his washed face, and I tidied his hair. He relaxed.

"I know, Isaiah," I said.

He started to cry, and I hugged him. I quickly turned his emotions to joy when I told him that if he ate the non-crumby parts, we could go to the park.

"How much time we got?" He meant with you.

"Hours." I smiled.

When you came in with Lily he was a different boy. He hammed for you and devoured his food. He asked you questions about everything, from bows and arrows to bears and wolves.

The dinners and the play became a routine. We came over on Friday and spent the night. You treated us well. You occasionally said some rude things to me, and you also guarded your time. Sometimes it was not a good day. I permitted it. Sometimes you were angry with me for asking you to text me more often. I permitted it. It was my fault, after all.

Every time there was a slight against me, I remembered when I reacted to your judgments with uncontrollable crying. I remembered when I hit myself until there were bruises on both sides of my head, and I also remember, somehow, those nights I slept better. Those nights, I wasn't convinced I was crazy. With you, in the newness of my medication and our agreements, I felt crazy.

I was so subdued. I was convinced that it was good

for me. And then you took my son to the park while I cooked something in your kitchen. You left your computer open so I could watch Netflix. There was an open document in the corner of the screen. A letter to a woman named Lillis.

You told her that your departure the other night was awkward. You apologized. You told her that you were not committed to anyone and that you did want to kiss her that night.

When you and my son came back, I was subdued. You would have called me crazy if I inferred too much from a letter about two friends having an awkward encounter. Friends can be attracted to each other. You had called her attractive in the past. I remembered that you told me your ex-girlfriend, the one you left *for me*, accused you of liking Lillis, and she was "crazy."

I breathed deeply and made jokes and held you. My son and I left the next day, and I did not hound you to see if you went straight to her.

I decided to give you an ultimatum on our next date. You and I were drunk in your bar. I had my hand wrapped around your wrist and my fingers couldn't clasp around it completely. I always marvel at your largeness. I was drunk and felt lighter than I normally do. I nonchalantly told you that, in three months, I was going to start seeing other people seriously.

"We can keep doing this. I know we kind of agreed not to fuck other people, but I want a relationship," I said.

"What?" You looked interested.

"Having sex. Not being serious. After three months I would like to try seeing other people."

We kept drinking, and my face was in such close proximity to yours the whole night. You are such a home to me.

"Three months," I said. I furrowed my eyebrows.

"Why?"

"What?"

"Why not now?" You said, really asking—as if you hadn't spent months explaining why.

"Now what?"

"We can do this now."

Because of my medication, I didn't cry over breakfast or minor transgressions. You believed me when I said the past was my fault. I believed me. When you were annoyed with me, I had to prove I was sane. I didn't speak my mind like I used to. You were beaming.

And then you told me that when Isaiah and I are to come for our weekly visit, you would be babysitting Lillis's dog. I said it was okay. You told me about the dog, and that it will eat gluten-free food. You didn't say anything about Lillis. I didn't either.

In my kitchen I turn the lights off again, like I used to. It allows me to feel as nothing as the dark. I know where everything is, like I did before. I become scared because it is this behavior that causes me to commit myself. I still take a knife and I press it against the fat of my palm—in the dark, hoping that I have the bravery to puncture myself, so that the next day I can be more fearless.

I was polite enough, and considerate enough, to hurt myself like a secret. So you didn't need to question how this kind of crazy would hinder your work or your isolation.

I knew that someone else would have congratulated herself for being contained. I understood how things could be misunderstood. I knew that, whichever white woman you saw while I was in the hospital, she would have let you have friends. She would have trusted that growth hurt but that it redefined the boundaries of the relationship— those boundaries were mutually developed in her mind. She would have convinced herself that permissiveness equated to a voice—like you wouldn't have fucking done what you do anyway, regardless of her consent or mine.

I turned the light on, and I had not punctured my skin. It was just the cutest red dot that stayed for several minutes—perfectly circular.

I called you. You seemed busy. I told you that I didn't want you to babysit Lillis's dog. You swore. You said that I could not do this. I couldn't tell you that it was impermissible after agreeing. You told me she was traveling, and it was not what friends did to each other. Your word mattered.

"I don't give a fuck. Fuck her. I don't like it," I said.

You yelled at me and hung up. I cried. You didn't call me back. I know that you felt in the right, because you assumed I had no knowledge of the awkward encounters you had with her. If you had known I knew, you would have had to acknowledge you were committed to me, and I had reason to dislike it.

I call you back after consoling myself. I told you it was fine.

You were so lukewarm the next few days. Those days were heavy for me. I asked my friends what I should do, and it was a unanimous, "Fuck Casey." Someone said I held some power in my secret knowledge. I told her it felt like the opposite.

Isaiah and I arrived at your house, and you had already started dinner. Rose, Lillis's dog, was running around. She looked like a white woman's dog. She was a blond mutt and looked like the type of dog that was meant to be roadkill, but rescue missions for stupid dogs interfered with the natural world.

I was still contained. You sensed anger. You knew I didn't like the dog or Lillis, but you also knew I had no real reason to be so angry (withholding the letter).

I tried to watch TV, and, behind the couch, the dog shat plainly on the wood floor. I told you to get rid of it. You began to clean, and then I resigned.

I was not going to be Laura or Lillis or Lily. I stood in the kitchen while Isaiah played in the furthest room away. You came to me.

"I read a letter where you said you wanted Lillis."

"I didn't say I wanted her," you said.

"You said you wanted to kiss her."

"We've been friends for years, and it was momentary. I'm not attracted to her."

It went back and forth, and you were never really sorry. You compared your transgressions to mine. I am erratic and cruel sometimes. The medication helped, I argued. I would have argued that the woman I was, outside of the hospital, deserved better.

We found solace in getting drunk together. At your bar, I told you that I wanted to be chosen. You explained that you were sorry. You told me that you chose me.

After last call, you told the doorman that we were going to make a baby in a pecan field.

We both stumbled on dirt roads to pick the most lush and soft field. We couldn't stop laughing. I believed, on this occasion, I was two inches taller than I had ever been. My body was rushing with newness and safety. You laid your coat down, and it was too dark for us to be soft and prepared. I saw your eyes and smiled before you kissed mine closed. We knew there would be a baby, as sure as we knew our love felt impossible and necessary.

The truth of this story is a detailed thing, when I'd prefer it be a symbol or a poem—fewer words, and more striking images to imbue all our things. I can't turn it into

Salish art. I had to fill these pages with the story of our new family, because the merging was so complicated, even I was confounded. I had to write full sentences, and the exposition lent itself to the dialogue, and there can't be ambiguity in the details of this story.

For you, and our child, and my sons, I said what happened up and down on the page. Because, if my sons want to see how terrible our love was, and why we chose it, they can see us closest here.

5

YOUR BLACK EYE

AND MY BIRTH

Pregnancy didn't stabilize our relationship. The baby was a Thunder Being inside of me. His growing cells and tissue heightened my awareness and physically incapacitated me.

He took the best parts of my blood. I became anemic.

I told you that I could not take my medication anymore. The risk to the baby was too much. You told me that you were prepared for it to be hard. *We want the baby*. We decided that Isaiah and I would move in with you.

The night at the pecan field amused us at doctor visits and ultra sounds. We always found a quiet moment to look at each other and laugh. There were good omens of our new family. We walked through a greenhouse with Isaiah. The smallest pots with little sprouts made us feel sentimental. You almost cried when you gave Isaiah a stuffed animal from your childhood: Charlie Chips, a puppy dog. He carried it with him everywhere. Your mother gave us things to decorate the baby's room.

It only took four weeks for the symptoms to appear. I yelled at my son in a way I never had, for no reason. I had the sense to apologize.

"Hormones," I said.

"Yeah. Dad Casey told me," he said, forgiving.

"You know that nobody, not even me, has the right to speak to you that way, no matter what you do?" I started to cry.

"I know, Mom," he said. He got himself a soda and sat with me on the couch in silence.

The work for my graduate program required me to generate prose and read more than I ever had. I also taught composition, and I didn't miss a day. When I was in the hospital, feeling crazy, I learned how to manage my symptoms in the external world. The techniques for coping worked outside. In the house, I was unsure how to cope. I wanted to cry, and hurt people, and I didn't trust myself. I didn't know if what I felt was authenticity, or a disease that would overtake me.

I wasn't sure I could control my behaviors. My disease was not an excuse to harm you, I knew.

My eating disorder became something else. I ordered every food I had starved myself of. My weak, and easily bruised, deficient body became thicker, like cedar bark or a trunk.

I started to ask you what you meant after you said anything. I started to scratch the back of my scalp, nervously, until I broke the skin. I refused to heal over, and pulled the scales from my open wound.

I began to tell you, often, that we were only a family because you chose me on a drunken night—because it seemed like a solution to a fight neither of us could ever win: Do you love me enough? Can I be good to you? I won't ever put a toilet seat up. You told me to stop.

My aunt said that being in the desert, away from my land, made me sick.

"Go to the river," she said.

"I will," I said, knowing I couldn't.

I couldn't distinguish the symptoms from my heart. It was polarizing to be told there was a diagnosis for the behaviors I felt justified in having. And then, I knew some part of my disease was spiritual or inherited.

I had not stopped wanting to die. It was not romantic because it felt passionless—like a job I hated and needed. Romanticism requires bravery and risk. The obsessive thoughts ruined things. Good news was met with a numb feeling. The voice I heard was practical. It noted every opportunity to die and then noted how I refused to jump out of a moving car. I refused to take all the pills I could find. I refused to drink myself to death. I refused to cut my pregnant body. I refused to buy a gun. I refused to crash my car. And I refused to jump from a spaghetti interchange. I was aware of every opportunity I missed.

I remembered when I thought I could go through with it. I remember being caught slumped against my bathroom door. My friend stuck his finger inside my throat until I purged. I remember waking up with blood and bile in my mouth. My friend said that he just knew I wasn't okay. It was strange because I didn't know. I had called him several times crying before that, and I can't remember how I had such conviction that day.

I was not right to want to die. I didn't want to leave my family. I liked my mind and its potential. I knew the type of burden I was. I was like my mother.

I have tried not to call her *my mother*. I started to believe that a person cannot own land or a family member.

"Where is your mother?" A woman asked me at a church thrift store. I was very small.

The woman took me to look for her, and, when Mom was found, she got angry at the white woman for chiding her.

In another store, I was accidentally locked in a bathroom stall in pitch black. I had gone to the bathroom, and a cashier came into the restroom and cleaned it. I sat silently in my stall, and my feet dangled from the toilet seat. I was too small to be seen. She turned the light off and closed the door. I heard a lock. Mom used to shop until stores closed. Eventually, someone let my mother in to look for me. They turned on the light, and I don't think I spoke. Nobody asked why I didn't speak. Nobody asked me what I did while I was in the dark. My mother didn't feel like *mine* as much as I wanted to belong to *her*—to be inseparable from her.

She taught me that I didn't own things. I really liked the idea of possession. We don't own our mothers. We don't own our bodies or our land—maybe I'm unsure. We become the land when we are buried in it. Our grandmothers have been uprooted and shelved in boxes, placed on slabs of plastic, or packed neatly in rooms, or turned into artifact—all after proper burials. Indians aren't always allowed to rest in peace. I want to be buried in a bone garden with my ancestors someday. I'd like to belong to that.

"If we can't die right, how are we gonna live right?" *my* mother would have asked.

Isaiah needs me more than ever. I tell him that you only want white women. I frighten him and you. There is a reason to live better now, I think, but I can't. The things I say to you both feel awful. I hear Mom in my own voice.

She is not all wrong. I'm carrying a child by a man who abandoned me for being too emotional and then got me pregnant. My emotions are unreasonable, you say.

You talk to me like you're teaching rhetoric.

"You're making leaps," you say. "There are more pleasant ways of asking what you need from me."

You carefully explain the semantics of your letter to Lillis. You decide for both of us that, given my transgressions, yours pale in comparison.

My language strengthened through all this discourse.

I asked myself if you chose me, or chose the woman I was when I was medicated. We fought until you had to leave me alone, pregnant, with Isaiah. I panic when I'm alone with him. I turn into the woman I was when Isadore was taken away.

I had always risen to the occasion of Isaiah, eventually, but in your home I couldn't stop crying. I have every trauma to pull from, to justify my fear that you don't really love me.

You come back to the door to explain how you choose me every day. I only respond with questions.

"Then why did you leave me in the hospital? What has changed since then, besides my pregnancy?"

I really want to know, and you can't explain. So, I can't feel safe. I can hear my aunt's voice, telling me that if my security depends on a man's words or action, I've lost sight of my power. I feel like I become worse, the more I know you love me. We are both worse for loving each other, it seems. It can get better. Descending to ascend—they call it. Everything feels ugly, and we are only at three months' gestation.

I plan for a trip to my low residency program in Santa Fe. We sent Isaiah, alone, on a flight to stay with Vito and Isadore for the weeks I'll be at IAIA.

♥

I searched your computer and saw that you told Lillis that the world was better with her in it, while I was in a hospital with brochures about my potential disorders. You had never told me before that the world was better with me in it, and I wouldn't have believed it either.

I found a conversation between you and Lily, where she asked what happened between you and me. You said I was a "cool girl," but it was just over. You were still fucking me, though.

You asked her if she wanted to hang out, not in a lecherous way. You are a great friend to women.

She told you that she had a problem with a man.

You told her you were a good listener.

Then, every Sunday, even after you and I made the commitment to a new fidelity, Lily goes to your house at night to smoke weed and watch TV. I learned, through the transcripts of your conversation, that moments after my son and I left your house, she was with you. I could not stop obsessing.

I explained to my friends that I don't think you slept with her. The strange thing is they believed me. I guess I was convincing.

The knowledge proposes I either start each day as new and take you for your word, or I tear the walls down to illustrate my pain. I feel pregnant with burden, and I chose it. I want to take it back.

I broke every glass. I broke windows. I threw out your possessions. You didn't apologize. You explained what a friendship is. You explained that, while she asked to cuddle you, you didn't proposition her.

The only thing, socioeconomically, practically, or rationally, I can do, is ask if you could abstain from speaking to her again.

The next day, I looked at the wreckage of our home. You forgave me with a resignation I saw in your face.

It had rained, and your chess pieces were already buried in the soil of our backyard.

We drove to Santa Fe, aware of my fragile state. You gave me your phone to look up directions in the middle of our long drive. Instead, I saw messages you sent to your Laura.

She wanted to see you months back. You explained to her that you would stop by after you visited your ex-girlfriend in the hospital, me.

And, to my surprise, you told her that you missed the smell of her on your pillow. The thing you told me the first nights we were together.

The first night you ever cooked for me, probably the way you cooked for her, you told me you loved me. I believed, after seeing how familiar you were with her, that your love was a slimy reproduction.

While I cried—while you drove—I punched you. You didn't swerve, but you held your eye with one hand. I cried over your reprimands. I cried over your shock, for hours, until we arrived at the hotel.

Because I can function in the external world, I showered and went to my first workshop at school. You drove me, because you feared I would hurt myself. You followed me in, because I asked you.

It was an Indian renaissance. Somehow it was more Indian with you there behind me, with a black eye. Somehow it was more Indian because I was pregnant. There was a medicine wheel in the academic building, so large and proud to be Indian that I knew I was home. There were Indian writers, and we smiled at each other, as if this was a sovereign land and we belonged.

You were a bystander to my joy. You had a black eye, and we covered it with excuses.

It was then I realized I was partly my father. I hurt you because I felt justified. You deserve a body without violation.

At residency, you did harmless things. When I came out of my first workshop, you were talking to a woman: a memoirist, who wrote about being a dominatrix. When I approached you both, you immediately introduced me. She asked you for your full name. She did not ask me for mine.

When we got home, she had already sent you a request to be friends on social media.

"This is what writers do. They network," you said.

That night my brother told me on the phone that Indian women were crazy, and white men never expect it. He told me I was not my father. We lamented together about the past.

He explained that my father was much worse than punches. Our father didn't like our brother Guyweeyo:

the oldest brother from another father. Our protector. He often punished Guyweeyo by pulling him into a room and locking the door behind them. We all have problems from that time. Problems I forget: We wet the bed as toddlers and children. I couldn't go to people's homes because of my accidents. The problem followed me into the third grade. None of us attended school frequently. All of us had substance abuse problems, which are still welcome over the very sober pain of remembering. Ovila told me that he doesn't know what our father did to Guy.

We lamented about Isadore. When Isadore was taken away, I often held newborn Isaiah, incapable of looking at him.

We remembered the night I took a bottle of aspirin, thinking I could kill myself. I told him that, in my sleep, I reached my arm over to pull Isadore closer to me in bed, and he was not there. I was terrified in the dark, searching with both hands to find my son. It took moments, maybe minutes, for me to realize that he was gone. He had been taken away.

I walked into the living room and Ovi was sitting down, holding a cup of tea. I didn't want to burden him with my pain. I think I forgot that Isaiah was even in his crib asleep. My pain was selfish.

I went into the bathroom and swallowed a bottle of aspirin. It was funny then, somehow, because Mom had only died several months before: her douche and hair dye and tweezers were still in the bathroom. I had to search through her things to find the bottle.

I told Ovi what I did, and he laughed at me. He

said that I should go and barf, because aspirin isn't fatal. He went to get me water, and, before he could return, I ran to the bathroom and made it to the sink. I threw up slimy, smaller white pills.

I had to hold myself against the walls to return to bed. My stomach hurt so much. My C-section scar ached. I laid down on my back, and he opened my door. He sat down and observed me.

He smiled as I groaned.

"Do you need an aspirin?" he said.

It was the most painful laugh. I remembered my new baby in the crib, who slept every night like clockwork, like a gift.

Ovila nursed me to health, and I nursed my baby. He made barbeque ribs and bought me pastries and served me orange juice. We had never had a relationship where either of us showed affection. He nursed me back into motherhood.

He nursed me back into leaving the house and taking adult education classes. When I realized the reservation was an insufficient place to learn, he let me leave without argument or concern.

I drank your beer in the hotel room in Santa Fe. You literally waited on the other side of the door for me. When I opened it, I had to face that I was part monster. I cried, and you didn't ask me to apologize, you didn't direct attention to the broken vessels on your face, the large black eye.

The next day at school I was pale from not sleeping and sick of myself.

After the residency, when we got home, I drove to a parking lot and called an abortion clinic. They immediately allowed me to speak with a doctor. I explained the situation: I am violent, I have hit myself in the face to cope with worthlessness, I hit you, and I wanted to die. I wanted to take pills I still had from before I was pregnant. Also, I want to live.

The doctor said she was confident that, given my circumstance, a late-term abortion would be considered necessary. I asked her for the price, and she directed me to the receptionist. It was roughly four hundred dollars, if, after consultation, it was approved.

I called you to ask for the money, and, instead, you pled for the baby's life. I hung up. I was familiar with the baby's life, but I couldn't think of that. I made more calls to foundations for women, clinics, groups, and then called back the same doctor. I was willing to sell my car or anything to have sanity again.

"When does my baby have bones?" I asked.

"This is something we should talk about in the consultation," the woman said.

I knew immediately that the Thunder Being inside of me had good bones. I thought of the bones from my lineage, which had been cemented inside the walls of residential buildings. I thought of my ancestors. I hung up and drove home.

In the next weeks, our baby in my womb reminded me of my brother Guyweeyo: willful and scared.

He kicked before the doctors predicted he would. He hiccupped each night at eleven.

I believed my mother spoke to our baby in my sleep. I think they devised a way to punish me for even thinking that a Thunder Being inside of me could be bad.

For a hundred days, it felt like Baby Guy was crawling out of my throat. I heaved until my face became blotchy. We believed it was an allergic reaction, but our doctor said it was blood vessels bursting from the strain of puking so often and so hard. No pill worked against the nausea.

I realized, after looking at my silhouette, seeing our small person expanding my reflection, that pain didn't burden me. Trying to forget damaged me the most.

Your eye has long since healed. I chose to be lethargic instead of angry in the last months of our pregnancy. Each night, I rested my head in your lap, and you placed your hand on my stomach. He kicked you, and I felt my mother raising her hands to me in the way Salish women do in ceremony, to say "thank you."

When the day came, I wasn't sure I was in pain enough, because the baby had conditioned me so well. We went into the hospital anyway, and Casey Guyweeyo was cut out from me, larger than he should have been. His skin is milk, and his body feels electric and unforgiving. He seems like the child my brothers, my sister, and I—could have been.

6

I KNOW I'LL GO

My father died at the Thunderbird Hotel on Flood Hope Road. According to documents, he was beaten over a sex worker or a cigarette. I prefer to tell people it was over a cigarette. I considered an Indian death myself, while walking along the country roads of my reservation, before I really considered life. His death intruded, as I could not fathom being a good person when I came from such misery.

I found newspaper clips about my father. Ken and four men abducted a girl. There aren't any details. There are documents about his murder and the transitional housing program he was in when he died. He was homeless, and social welfare gave him a hotel room, next to sex workers and younger, more violent men. There was nothing easy about his memory or what he left behind.

He was an anomaly, a drunk savant. He took his

colors, brushes, and stool when he left my mother. It was harvest, and the corn stalks were gold and waving. I was constantly waiting outside on the porch. I ate blueberries and spit out anything too ripe—a purple liquid. I remember staring at my spit on the porch.

His hair was black and coarse. He was wearing a baseball tee shirt and jeans covered in rust acrylic.

As an Indian woman, I resist the urge to bleed out on a page, to impart the story of my drunken father. It was dangerous to be alone with him, as it was dangerous to forgive, as it was dangerous to say he was a monster. If he were a monster, that would make me part monster, part Indian. It is my politic to write the humanity in my characters, and subvert the stereotypes. Isn't that my duty as an Indian writer? But what part of him was subversion?

Our basement smelled like river water and cedar bough. He carved and painted endlessly in the corners of the room. While I sat in his lap, he taught me our icons. Eagle was Mother, and bolts were Thunder Being, and his circles were the universes. It meant so much to draw a circle well. He practiced and let me watch. I remember when he left, my mother started to paint again. I remember that, while my father tried to draw a circle with his own eyes and hands, my mother used coffee cans. I resisted the iconography and found myself more interested in why Salish work wasn't true to life.

My therapist asked me to speak to my father and mother in a session. I told my father that a bird is just a bird. A mother is a tangible thing. Making Indian women inhuman is a problem for me. We've become too symbolic and never real enough.

My therapist asked me to speak to my mother and I couldn't.

My father was soft looking sometimes. I liked to sleep in the crook of his neck. He smelled like Old Spice and bergamot. His hands shook when he was not drinking, at his worst. And when I held his hands he seemed thankful. He delighted in my imagination. The grass was always high in our lawn, and he often let me use the hose to fill buckets and wash tires—I pretended it was a snake.

My mother wanted to heal him. I remember several trips to visit him in rehab. She sent him to islands, and I remember wearing a lifejacket, crossing water to somewhere in Tofino, British Columbia. I remember each hope given to me by my mother: that our father would be okay and things would be different.

In the past, I wanted to tell her that some things can't be loved away, but I think she knew that.

We left my father a few times. We stayed in my uncle's home. Mom took all four of us, along with my grandmother. We all slept in one room, and I had chicken pox. I slept in a green upholstered chair and had an accident. My brother Ovila was the only one awake. He told me to undress and took off his shirt for me to wear. I went back to sleep with a sour stomach and woke up as my father was forklifting me from the chair to his van. He always found us.

Once, I packed my bags, mimicking my mother.

With a bag of dolls and wooden cars, I told him I was leaving. I told him I would not come back until he stopped drinking.

"Come here," he said.

"No," I said.

He promised me he would quit and then left.

My brothers told me that he didn't really leave. I misremembered. My grandmother saved money and asked our cousin to kill my father. The man beat him well, and, when my father came home, we were gone. He ruined every artwork we possessed. He tossed every can of salmon and beets that my grandmother had prepared for the winter. He took jewelry and money.

When we got home, everyone told me to wait on the porch. They went inside and cleaned while I stared at my spit. For years, they were happy to let me imagine he left on his own regard.

After my mother died, I went to find him. He lived in a town called Hope. He had a new family, and our van sat in his front lawn on bricks. When he answered the door, he told me he knew who I was. He had a thin, dirty white shirt on. He looked ill, and his face was gaunt. His hair was still black in some parts.

His wife, Winnie, was my older sister's childhood friend. My father had met her when she was a girl, visiting my sister. After years with Ken, her front teeth were gone. She smiled at me and said my father had old videotapes of theater work I had done in the community. I had five new brothers, so young. They looked like the archetypes my own family had formed in the presence of my father. I found myself in the youngest child, who formed bonds too quickly and needed holding.

My father and I sat across from each other in lawn chairs in his basement. I resisted the urge to sit poised like him. Instead, I held bad posture and slunk in my chair.

"You have my nose," he said.

I said I missed him, feeling awful that it was true.

"The best thing I could do was leave."

"I know," I said.

"Your mother was a good woman. I told her I was an asshole, and she took me in—like a wounded bear."

"I know," I said.

A month after this, he showed up at my house with a white documentary filmmaker. I answered the door but could not let him in the house. My brother Ovila was still scared of him, still angry and confused.

"They're doing a documentary about me," he said. "About my art."

I was anxious, standing there with him at my door.

"I know," he said. "I'll go."

I hugged him in my driveway. I know that the whole rez was watching, even my sister, who knocked on my door after he left to look me in my eyes so I could see that I betrayed her. Even she, who was as tall as him, and bigger, had to come to my door with backup. Even she was scared of him. I didn't know any better back then.

The National Film Board of Canada debuted the documentary as a piece with immediacy and no external narrative. I'm a woman wielding narrative now, weaving the parts of my father's life with my own. I consider his work a testimony to his being. I have one of his paintings in my living room. "Man Emerging" is the depiction of a man riding a whale. The work is traditional and simplistic. Salish work calls for simplicity, because an animal or man should not be convoluted. My father was not a monster, although it was in his monstrous nature to leave my brother and I alone in his van while he drank at The Kent. Our breaths became visible in the cold. Ken came back to bring us fried mushrooms. We took to the bar fare like puppies to slop.

His smell was not monstrous, nor the crooks of his body. The invasive thought that he died alone in a hotel room is too much. It is dangerous to think about him, as it was dangerous to have him as my father, as it is dangerous to mourn someone I fear becoming.

I don't write this to put him to rest but to resurrect him as a man, when public record portrays him as a drunk, a monster, and a transient.

I wish I could have known him as a child in his newness. I want to see him with the sheen of perfection, with skin unscathed by his mistakes or by his father's.

It's in my nature to love him. And I can't love who he was, but I can see him as a child.

Before my mother died I asked her if he had ever hurt me.

"I put you in double diapers," she said. "There's no way he hurt you. Did he ever hurt you?"

"No," I said.

If rock is permeable in water, I wonder what that makes me in all of this? There is a picture of my brother, Ovi, and me next to Dad's van. My chin is turned up, and at the bottom of my irises there is brightness. My brother has his hand on his hip, and he looks protective standing over me. I know, without remembering clearly, that my father took this picture and that we loved each other. I don't think I can forgive myself for my compassion.

7

LITTLE MOUNTAIN WOMAN

I feel like a squaw. The type white people imagine: a feral thing with greasy hair and nimble fingers wanting. My earliest memories, and you, and the baby, have turned earth in my body. I don't know what I am anymore.

You have made me feel sick of myself.

I killed a ladybug when we were walking, and you looked at me like I was wild. I am the mother of your son. I don't think you know how poor I used to be—that my house was infested with ladybugs for so long. My brother and I went mad when they wouldn't stop biting. We tried to swat them with brooms and towels. We tried to corner them. Their death smelled like a puddle and wouldn't leave our home. My mother didn't come home when the bugs overtook the living room. She was working three days on and three days off, and, between that, she was with Larry: my sister's father, who resurfaced in her life, twenty years too late. Just in time for my mother's midlife crisis.

I don't think you know how poor that made me feel, a squaw child.

I kill ladybugs whenever I see them. I know that the women you've loved wouldn't do that. They consider the things lucky. So much of the world shames me.

I never get to say the full thing with you. Like the ladybugs. I don't think you know how I feel. That having the baby didn't make things better.

Before I went to the hospital, I drove to your home—at night. It was December in Mesilla. My moist hand stuck to your door.

You pulled me in, and we stumbled to your couch. We sat for minutes in silence, beyond polite conversation, in the dark.

I felt like a voyeur, staring at everything you owned. I wanted things to be mine too. You wouldn't keep someone like me. I think you wanted the other women you were seeing—whole beings.

My thighs were sweaty, and your heater was buzzing. The skin on my neck parted away from itself like arid soil.

Your hands were holding themselves in your lap. You wore old clothes that stayed too long in the corners of your floor. You were dusty, and I liked that.

You've said before that I'm mercurial. I don't know.

89

Pain feels faster than light. I react to pain, and there's too much of it.

In my first marriage, I was a teenager. I got married to leave my mother's house because foster care didn't work. I had aged out. I left to prove I could leave, and then I had Vito's baby. And then my mother died. I flew home to be in the room when they pulled the plug. He came with me, and we brought our son Isadore.

After her funeral, we stayed in my mother's duplex and packed her boxes. She had left the house I grew up in because it was infested with mold. During renovations, reckless kids broke in and, in some drunken dialogue, burned the house down.

My ex-husband and I pushed each other—yelled at each other. And Isadore just rattled the gate at the stairway and sat in corners waiting for me. He was born gifted and moved silently throughout my world—unsure if he could trust me. He was a little ghost like I was to my mother. Little ghosts don't carry little wounds. I think our pain expands the longer we're neglected.

I got pregnant again by Vito. People have a right to think things will change. I allowed myself that much.

The tips of your fingers felt like wet grapes. I wanted to bite every one. I told you that I needed help, and you asked me to leave. A friend of yours had just taken his own life. It seemed unforgivable that I would be suicidal or wild when you needed me. I know at my worst I appear disposable, or that I make myself that way.

❤

My first husband kept me awake at night, knowing I had to work the next day. I argued until I fell asleep in bed, and he appeared above me with a knife. My blinds were open, and, in the dark, I saw the moonlight catch his blade. He didn't speak to me. When I started to move he left the room.

The next day I told him to leave, and then I begged him, and then I hit him hard enough to compel him to run.

I committed myself after you asked me to leave. The nurses gave me a composition book and a ballpoint pen: the least I was ever given to write with, and I produced so much work. Every letter was to you. I don't think you know what your word meant to me. I found hundreds of ways to ask you if I was wrong. I tried to ask you, without your pride, was our problem your fault at all? Were you really cold, or do I just imagine people don't care about me?

When I got out, I could read the dark. I turned the lights off in my kitchen and walked across the tiles. I had cleaned the room several times, and it became lonelier as each speck was wiped clean. I felt absent without you or the dirt. Even my ghosts left me.

I wondered if your hands were still cold. You reminded me of a broken spring–rocking horse, and I was all weight.

Vito called the police after I hit him. I called my sister. When the cops came, they asked what I did to my husband. I wasn't sure. Isadore sat in my sister's lap. The officers asked me to show them my wrists.

They reassured me that Vito had no marks where I had hit him—and that he would be fine.

I pulled back my sleeves and there were small, thin, red lines across my wrists. My sister cried and held her mouth. She had seen worse, and I expected more from her. I knew that cutting myself was wrong. I was pregnant and a mother.

I reappeared in your life, and you were still seeing other women. I feel sick of myself when I consider my agency with you.

A woman you liked played the banjo, the one with the gluten-free dog.

When I feel like a squaw, I wash my face with alcohol—toner. There's never enough dirt to constitute the compulsion to clean myself or think I'm dirty.

My ex-husband's family had an endless bankroll for lawyers and detectives, and I spent most of my pregnancy in court, trying to retain custody of Isadore.

"You were in foster care?" my lawyer asked.

"Yes. Can they use that against me?" I asked.

"Everything is fair game."

In moments like that, I remembered the ladybugs and mold. I remembered sour meat in the fridge and needing Mom to come home. I remembered what it was like to be nothing.

She came home after three weeks once. I screamed at her for leaving my brother and me. I told her that I would take off with my boyfriend if she didn't change. She unplugged the landline phone, so I couldn't call anyone, and locked it in her bedroom with her padlock.

I remember, when she left, kicking down the door. I called a social worker who had been sniffing around. I was glad to bring the shame to our home. I was glad to expose her.

What they didn't tell me was that I wouldn't see my brothers if I stayed in care. Maybe visits, my social worker told me when I asked. Before I turned eighteen, child protective services let me go home, after four different types of foster families. After I realized dysfunction was too well ingrained, I couldn't stand each family's specific type of awful or safe.

A woman you liked left tennis balls at your place. I searched through your phone and found pictures of her dog. It was a small terrier with white fur. I don't know why she didn't send pictures of herself. I know that you liked that.

How you fucked me then was degrading. I knew that when you were done you were also finished with me. The other women, white women, were treated like good friends. I could have used that.

One morning, I left your house, and you saw me later in public. You didn't stop to speak to me. You waved.

Maybe I make myself the squaw? Maybe, this whole time, I should have sent you pictures of my hands.

I was not the mother Isadore deserved. I was distant and kept to a routine, so that there were no moments of candid and inexplicable love. I won in provincial court, and supreme, and then we had a date for the Hague Convention.

My lawyer tried to explain what it was. She told me a story about a woman who abducted her child from Ireland to escape her husband. The Hague Convention deported the child back to Ireland.

"What did the mother do?" I asked.

"I think she moved back to Ireland."

Isaiah didn't move in the womb. My doctor told me some babies were quiet and lazy.

The things you said to your white women—I wanted that.

I slouched and inhaled shorter breaths to take up less space around you. I understood I had sacred blood, but what would that mean to a white man like you? I know. I know the tenses and the syllables of every rite and had spent hours with women who made medicine. I wasn't made to be ornamental, but it's what I wanted. I inherited black eyes and a grand, regal grief that your white women won't own or carry. I don't think you know how I felt, and I wondered what my grief looked like to you?

I went into labor alone in the hospital. I gave birth alone. I held Isaiah in my arms. When my lawyer said Isadore would be taken away soon, deported back to the U.S., Isaiah was in my arms.

"I don't understand. I have my baby," I said.

"I told them they would be separating brothers, and about your culture, and no one said you were unfit," my lawyer said.

"What happened?"

"Isadore was born in America, and Vito said that he was coerced into leaving with you and his son to Canada. The convention is international. That's a concern."

"What about this boy?" I asked.

"They don't seem interested yet," she said.

I went back to get my earrings from your house and saw you holding your Laura in the doorway. I still knocked.

You told me to come back later.

How many times did I go back before I got pregnant? When did I become enough for you, and what was the distinction? It would help to know what makes me worthwhile, and what doesn't.

♥

I sent Isadore Hot Wheels cars in the mail. I cradled Isaiah and couldn't look at him. I wasn't sure if I had a right to be a mother if I had no right to have Isadore. It didn't make sense.

My therapist guided me and showed me how to hold Isaiah. She made me look him in the eyes and explained he wasn't bonded to me. He averted his gaze when I was close, as if I were a monster. I know I am a squaw.

Social workers offered me respite—time away from my baby. I used the time to drink. I didn't think it was possible to be fortunate enough to be a mother again.

Isaiah cried all night, and I remembered well that I held a hand over his mouth, long enough for me to know I was a horror to my baby. Nobody wanted him for those split seconds, and I wondered why the people who should be punished the most aren't punished. Because they hurt children who don't matter.

After those seconds of postpartum depression, or grief, or terror, I took the transgression to healers and social workers and therapists. They absolved me—what else do they expect from someone like me, I thought.

One woman, the director of the Health Department, said I was a tiger cornered in a room. My circumstance was a cage. My marriage was a prodding thing, and my baby was still my cub. I don't excuse myself, even when the analogies align.

I was lucky to get a ride into town to give birth—and social workers had to drive Isaiah and me home from the hospital. I often looked at him and wondered if we existed. I answered the question by saving my checks and taking night classes. I answered the question by leaving the reservation for any other place. Someone offered to share an apartment in El Paso, in the desert. I went.

I can't believe my reserve of water—from my nose and eyes. I have dormant fluid in my body, every woman does. I don't know if I am a cavern or a river.

Once, you said I was a geyser: a hole in the ground—bursting.

Pain is faster than light, and I wish people would not fault me for things I can't forget or explain.

When I became pregnant, your women fell away. Your fingers were less edible. I had our baby boy, remembering the women and my sons. White women have always made me feel inferior, but I don't think you know how much. All you see is me killing ladybugs, or crying, or asking you what I did. You can't know the spite of my feelings.

I sold everything to come to America: my ex-husband's Beanie Babies (which his mother asked for in the divorce), my wedding ring, my bike, my mother's broken car, and her winter jackets.

I made the active choice that my son and I were real. I held him while I cooked, and I didn't clean very often so I could keep him in my arms. He fit well on my hip and learned to keep his small hands inside the neck of my shirt for comfort. He asked for bottles by putting his fingers in my mouth. He became expressive. He laughed at everything. We saw each other more than the world could see.

You and I compare hurt. I only feel dirty every day and some nights. I wash my face three or four times, and, when I told you I wanted to be pore-less, you told me people should have pores.

I feel dormant watching you live fuller than I can. I worry I am a cavern. I've inherited my mother's hollow stomach.

You tell me that my pain feels searing and that I'm missing four layers of skin. Your pain is an empty room. I agree.

When I was eleven, I stared in the mirror to see if I had breasts yet. Fred Cardinal, an elder, was in the next room. He called me in and said, "Your name is Little Mountain Woman: Asiniy Wache Iskwewis." I felt ashamed and undeserving of the name. He wanted me to know that I was good and holy, but I didn't think that my body was a universe. I didn't think I would unravel so well either. I drew power from the mountains and chose a home in the desert.

♥

When we got married, the officiant said it would be hard.

In marriage—swollen and postpartum, I stared at our bed, which was held up by books. I wanted to fix it. I stripped the bed more often than you liked. We washed the sheets. I stared at the doorway, where you held another woman once, and I saw myself on the other side—a squaw. I washed my face again and again and considered that, if you knew more about my pain, I might feel less of it.

I think you imagined I was sacred before you used me. My heart has an extra chamber now. I am more fragile than you know, more squaw and ornamental. I can turn my chin and pose like a figurine. I wonder how much you can know about being used? Can you wash me like a saint? From squaw, to mother with a face, and pores, and a body, and my own good history—I want my large heart, but older and safer, and clean. Can't you wash me? Or hollow me out for good? Wash me in my own regard and pain, and let me dry out. Let me kill every ladybug and laugh when I do. Don't leave me. I can't bear to lose my sons, or any more of myself, or you.

8

THE LEAVING DEFICIT

It's strange that, when I was scared to lose you, I chose
to leave you first. I left you and went to Barbara's.

We exchange gifts before I tell her why I left. I give
her a handcrafted silver ring wrapped in a mustard cloth.
She presents me with a sweetgrass braid as long as my
arm, still wet from the braiding. The gifts are ritual and
plenty—yellow roses and basil plants and tobacco and
books we like and things for ceremony.

She thinks my husband doesn't understand how to
communicate love, and I think he's impotent.

"White men," Barbara says.

"His anger just wells into nothing."

We give different theories to each other and con-
clude that maybe he's not the problem. Maybe there's no
problem, and I can't deal with that.

Every time I leave, my husband says that he can't make me stay. *Can't you*, I think, every time.

My mother and I found an eagle carcass on our way to the river. With the feathers plucked, we saw its sinewy skin.

"White men," Mom said.

Feathers are a gift and flexible protein. Mom put down tobacco and ran her fingers over its exposed parts. She told me the salmon run was coming, and this bird would have wanted for nothing.

She wanted me to see the deficit white people leave.

Nobody wants to know why Indian women leave or where they go. Our bodies walk across the highway from the dances of our youth into missing narratives without strobe lights or sweet drinks in our small purses, or the talk of leaving. The truth of our leaving or coming into the world is never told.

While my ancestors' bones laid proud and dull in the grave, or on display, mine were hot light ready to go.

Larry was my mother's worst boyfriend. He came into my life when I was sixteen. He started to walk across the halls naked. I thought he was a walking corpse. He played a ghost, looming between my mother and me. He went to the kitchen and never ate. His insides were rot. Drunks can't eat after a point. He drove me to school holding a beer can, a tangible thing in his unstable hand. My mother didn't believe me, so it was always an unreal taking. He touched me to help me out of the car.

I searched for irrefutable things to tell my mother. None of it compared to the days they went clamming together, or collected devil's club in the valley. My mother never liked the beach until Larry came around with his rake and gloves. They waded in gloomy water as I watched from the truck. They seemed content. It didn't matter if he groped me. It didn't matter if he groped my cousin. None of that mattered.

I told my mother that she might have stopped drinking before I was born, but she was still a drunk. She stopped bringing Larry home. Instead, they went to his place in the city. There were only so many places where men like him could live. I took a bus there to find her. I saw my mother differently.

Larry lived on the first floor in what I thought was a drug house. Women, girls like me, sat outside on couches with babies, stood inside the hallway, and made tea in the kitchen. I knocked on his bedroom door. My mother was ashamed, under the covers in his bed. She rummaged through her purse and handed him twenty dollars.

"Here," he said. "Go back to the rez."

This is how we go missing.

This is how we decide to leave.

I left on Valentine's Day after the dance. The hall wasn't decorated. The girls and I stood in circles in strobe lights and had sweet drinks in our small purses, and we had my talk of leaving.

"Fuck it," Lucy said. "Don't come back."

Lucy was shorter than all the Chehalis girls, but she walked up to them anyway to start shit. We left, drunk, and went out along the highway. The trucks honked at our silhouettes. Nobody wants to know how we leave. I only had one bag to pack, and I didn't have money. My boyfriend, Vito, let me live with him in his mother's home. It was better than foster care.

His whole family was large and Republican. I acclimated from my Marxist-Leninist mother to their lifestyle. We ate top sirloin and fried shrimp, and Bush became the president again. They asked me to vote and drove me to the polling station, and I went in and stood there long enough. Every day was like that for me.

I called my mother to show her I could leave.

"What are you going to do?" she asked.

"Not be there," I said.

"Where are you?" she asked.

When a man's hands become a ghost, there is no way to strip them from a body. Haunting, what a mother does not see. Native women walk alone from the dances of our youth into homes they don't know for the chance to be away. Their silhouettes walk across highways and into cars at night. They are troubled by nothing but the chance that they might have to come back someday to bury their mothers.

My mother died on Thanksgiving. My brother was watching *The Texas Chainsaw Massacre* in the next room. Larry was already dead from liver failure. I flew in from a place far removed. I worked for the Bureau of Indian

Affairs. I prayed over her body and touched her delicate skin. A bloat protruded from her neck, and I felt that too. I felt the deficit.

I took her house and its contents and let her ghost in. The people said to put away the pictures, but I didn't. They said to cover the mirrors, but I didn't. The ritual of death was not interesting. And then I left her home again.

I found humor in leaving.

I punctured a friend's chest with a fork. He heard me when I said no.

Another dug his knuckles into me. I didn't cover the marks. He gave me his credit card, and I bought diamonds and hammered silver.

Another, I left in the waiting room of his lawyer's office. He wanted to prove he didn't sleep with a student of his. The lie detectors—and his guilt—were enough for me. He gave me my first STD. He gave me three thousand dollars, and I bought summer classes. When I graduated, he asked for a picture, but I didn't reply.

Another, I left in Miami. He didn't think I was like that, but I was clearly like that. I only smiled at room service.

"What do you want?" I asked men, like an indictment.

Another has white guilt and thinks it's progress to bind me.

"Can you say all you want from me in one breath?" I asked.

♥

Barbara asks what I get in leaving. I tell her that my husband left me in the hospital once before we were married.

"I guess I took him back to leave him."

He visited me in the hospital for finality. Suicidal ideation troubled him too much. I asked if he felt culpable. There was a crafted tree on the walls for the sick women, made of paper and crayon and glue. The tree had leaves, thirty different colors, with words on them like "Intelligent," "Smart," "Brave," "Bold," "Strong" . . . Casey pointed to "Sexy." I put the leaf in my pocket and used it as a bookmark for a year.

Barbara tells me to go back. He doesn't hit me, she says. He's intelligent. We have a baby. The wet sweetgrass she braided is dry and straight. She puts it below the windshield in my car and when I drive back I'm not sure I will stay.

Her house is a lot of old pictures and plants and draped scarves. A blue budgie sings in her office, and there are a few old drums around. It is everything of my mother and home.

I hold my sons at night, and they are so still, like rocks. I run my fingers over their foreheads and wonder how they don't collect dust. Boys asleep, and I am a rare carcass in the river, bloated with deficit. Every time I see wings flap I think of leaving. It used to feel like breaking vertigo, and now it is just breaking.

♥

Now that I stay, we have the same fight.

"I'm trying not to be an asshole," you say.

"Sometimes trying to be the absence of something makes you that very thing."

I understand I am talking about myself and leaving. We can sit together for hours with the deficit, and it's not unusual anymore—it's ritual. Us both, trying to be the absence of something and forgiving each other for the children we have become. I think about my mother, knee deep in the beach with a rake, smiling at Larry. I think about myself, in the back of the truck, needing her. And after all of this there are still rocks in the old home I grew up in, the home that burned down. There are still lava sweat lodge rocks sitting underneath grass that overgrew a fire pit.

There is some stillness, even in my history—a good secret in so much bad. It almost feels like a betrayal to have good thoughts. Sometimes I know part of me is still a ghost, walking next to my mother, looking for something to make an offering to, holding her hand. Either this feeling means that part of me is dead, or that she's alive, somewhere inside of me.

9

THUNDER BEING

HONEY BEAR

I avoid the mysticism of my culture. My people know there is a true mechanism that runs through us. Stars were people in our continuum. Mountains were stories before they were mountains. Things were created by story. The words were conjurers, and ideas were our mothers.

Thunder is contrary. Thunder can intuit, and her action is the music caused by lightning. She comes because we ask, and that's why falling apart is holy.

People said I came from thunder. I thought the quick chaos was my master. My dreams were about a spinning wheel—symbols of an unstoppable force that would ruin me. I was a child when I told my mother there was a large wheel in my dreams. She asked me what I did when I saw it.

"I watched it," I said.

She looked at me carefully that day. She took out her paints and drew a thunderbird on a white poster board. Before the paint dried, I put my finger on its blue chest.

When I got my period, she gave me a Waterford crystal heart. I wore it like my brother wore his medicine bundle—around the neck and under the shirt. It felt like a new organ.

In a coffee shop, I couldn't catch my breath and doubled over with pain. I remembered a man in the shower. I went outside. Closing my eyes only disoriented me further from the world, and holding on to things made me feel too connected—receptive to every fiber or bench or tree. I called Casey.

I wondered if he thought this was a real emergency or another dramatic thing—I am constantly in some panic or despair, it seems. I worried more than I could breathe.

What do I do with my hands, I thought. What do I do with my eyes, which felt obscene in the light.

Thunder can awaken one's soul, even the atheist without. We have clowns in my culture, who carry a subversive nature. When women wail, or when they won't speak, a clown will throw its snot, or contort its body to point to how absurd our pain is—or how pointless it is to try to contain it. That contrary nature can awaken the dead.

I thought about my mother's body, weak. My father's body, jaundice. His pubic mound was black, and beneath the steam and soap, I can smell him—years away, I can smell him. I covered my nostrils. I remembered showering with my father, more than once, and I remembered my fear of breathing.

I had a new knowledge, or memory, and knew to be ashamed. The truth sometimes doesn't appear exact but approximate. I knew my own fingers and my father's were shameful. I remembered, in the coffee shop, something so brief and kinetic that I didn't want to be in my body. My father, in the bathroom, had asked me to shower with him when I was five or six.

Things connect with the right conduit: one right memory had been absent.

As a child, I had drawn in my journal a male figure, naked. My mother was shocked, so I told her a friend had drawn it. I was forbidden from going to the girl's house again, and my mother explained to me that men hurt children. They're capable.

"What Michelle drew," she said, "is not right."

She called Michelle's parents, and I remember thinking how right the drawing was. How I scaled each limb and part well enough that the girl next to the man appeared small, and her smile was not a real smile, but a sign. My mother, she believed my lie easily, without question. Not one.

♥

Thunder Being made me feel like I had forgotten ten thousand irons plugged in. I couldn't go home. I could only let things burn while I looked at my hands.

My husband held my shoulders.

"I don't know what to do with my hands," I said.

A graduate student approached us and ignored my eyes. I felt more present than I ever had, and invisible. It was Thunder Being's game, or a gift of memory. This was more than simple traumatic stress, or me, open and gawking at my true misery. I was the third generation of the things we didn't talk about.

Casey and I went to the car.

"Do you want a margarita?" he asked.

My husband. Six-four, large head, large blue eyes, hapless and already acclimated to the chaos of me. My calls and my anxiety and the idea that I might never be okay were acceptable by now—usual.

"It's okay to not be okay," a mentor had said to me once.

I held the armrests of the car, looking outside like a child, waiting for my body to feel organic again, like when I'm teaching: bouncing around the room with an agenda. At thirty-two I was a child, a victim of something. I saw his pubic mound in my mind. I was afraid of what that meant. Afraid that I might remember clearly what happened. I made a life out of naming things, and I couldn't speak this.

"I need to see someone about this," I said.

♥

The therapist tapped my kneecaps, one and then the other. I closed my eyes.

"What's your safe space?" she asked.

Her office was small. She was licensed, just enough to deal with my trauma, but not educated beyond my comprehension. She was not so smart that I would worry what she was writing in her notebook. Her hair was short. She scared me, with her aura, as someone who believed in God and would have me believe too if I wasn't mindful.

"My safe space is outside my childhood home." Outside in the yard, overlooking forty acres of corn. I liked the whistle of the stalks and loneliness. There were only coyotes in the field, and crows, and wild things— weaving through dry stalks.

My eyes moved back and forth as she tapped me, left and right. I felt like a pendulum, or something open, steady and drawing to a time. Ready to greet some horrible memory beneath the safety of my space.

"How is your stress?" she said.

Her name was Adrienne, like a poet I loved. A woman of exclusion, who loved women enough to give her work solely to them. Adrienne was part of a continuum working against erasure. I think my counselor was too, by letting me remember. I believe Indian women remember often, like me, but mostly it is while their hands are wrist deep in the dishes. There is always something on the floor to pick up with a rag—always a counter.

"Get a teddy bear," she said. "You'll want to let *her* pick it out." She pointed to my heart, indicating the child within me. "Hold it like you would hold yourself. Comfort yourself."

At Walgreens, the only one that struck me was a light brown bear who reminded me of honey. It had a bowtie. His head was bigger than my inner child's head. He reminded me of a bear my mother brought home from the Nechi Institute, a place where she studied to become a counselor.

During that time, she was very experimental. She'd test our tongues for candida, observing how white they were. She made us eat wild rice but never learned to cook it properly. She made us beat pillows, stuffed animals, and rugs when we misbehaved, because she wanted us to release our tensions. My brother and I could only laugh at her parental antics, unable to combat her theory, only able to see its silliness. It was all a response to Grandma dying, and my father leaving, and my tuberculosis.

She brought me a bear like the new one I found at Walgreens, and she told me she loved me. I might be misremembering the words, but I know that she meant to say she loved me. She loved dearly, and often gave me things to nurture. I received so many dolls, bears, and small animals before I became a woman.

The first time I held Honey Bear I was alone in my bedroom. I told him it was okay. I was here, and he was safe. I was part of a continuum against erasure, I told myself. My body felt stronger when I embraced it. I felt connected to a lineage of women who had illustrated their bodies and felt liberated by them. Thunder might have been within me the day I had coffee, freeing the memory of my father, revealing some chaos to me too quickly to comprehend.

"He's a good-looking bear," Casey said, observing it.

"It feels good to hold it."

When I was a little girl I had a dog named Buddy. His fur stood up in thunderstorms. His coat was all antennae. He used to fall asleep with his nose against my skin. I never let him sleep alone in storms. He was mauled by coyotes and survived.

After he recovered, he kept running away, and I felt like he was running away from me. There was a blue house down my street, where a German shepherd was chained up in the front. Buddy was cuddled up to that big dog. He was so small next to her. I pulled his body away from her by the collar, and he started to piss on me. I felt so betrayed. He was my only friend. It wasn't long after that—he ran away for good. The dog was something good and small and the first thing in my life I could hold. I remember that I confided in him that I had been hurt. I think he was the only one I told. I thought the burden of knowing was too much, and that's why he ran away. I'm still somehow convinced.

After I was gifted with approximate memory—after crying a few hundred times, Casey squeezed my hand,

and we kissed each other. I felt the sticky notes of my lips pull apart from his. The right love is an adhesive. I realized that I had a singular mind with Casey. Even with my duplicity and my rambling. I felt unworthy of that kind of love and ready for it.

"My father," I said.

Just saying the two words cracked my voice. It was enough for him to know.

"He hurt me," I said.

Just the three words were too many and enough for me to know.

The rest of the year was a practice in language. Every new word became more horrific. I can say full sentences. In the shower, before I knew how to be scared or protect myself, I disappeared. Ten minutes of my life were enough to kill me. Every day I negotiate the minutes of my life, remembering that I can't remember enough. I spend hours convincing myself that no child is ruined—and the one inside of me is worth remembering fondly. My mother's looming spirit guides me some days, telling me that nothing is too ugly for this world. I am not too ugly for this world.

10

INDIAN CONDITION

My education was a renaissance, and I know what comes after discovery. I graduated in a woven cedar cap and blue shawl. I was given a sovereign land to write every transgression.

When I walked across the stage, I remembered, some years ago, when Isaiah had lice. Doctors couldn't see the nits and told me I was just imagining things. I put two rooted teardrop eggs that were attached to my son's hair into a sandwich bag. The nurses looked at it closely and told me it could be nothing.

Only when I started to pick his scalp with my fingers, on the plane to America, did people seem to care or see. The entire flight, my hands worked and found each clinging thing. Isaiah was happy to be still, and happy to have my fingers acknowledge each exposed space—his follicles too. Every child deserves a type of servitude. He fell asleep and dreamed. I know because he salivated and murmured against my chest. When every tiny seed and itch was stripped, we landed, and he woke up.

I remember how well my work on his head was timed, and that America would be the beginning of our new life. I remember being ashamed to have groomed my baby like an animal on a flight filled with white people. I remember that motherhood is mostly bearing shame to dress my children, to feed them, and to spare them the things I wasn't spared.

I came to America because I lost my baby and had one in my care—to feed. I came because I didn't have my GED. I came because I was done with ghosts. It was all too ugly to say, until I received an education and walked across the stage.

A Native writer read my work and said, "It's no wonder that this narrator is crazy. She's Indian, and she's smart. Who could survive that?"

If the Institute of American Indian Arts was a renaissance, then this is what comes after discovery.

I became an editor. They pay me for my work. I became a *fellow*. Words I never knew to be—I am.

More than a drunken father or monster, and more than the bright of my iris, or the hope I was given from my grandmother. I've exceeded every hope I gave to myself.

I still hold my coffee, and remember until it runs cold.

When I hear empty bottles, I remember. Empties are a cliché—the sound of them is so familiar. The collective sound of glass against glass, muffled by brown paper bags and collapsing tin. Empties are my father and Larry.

Sometimes I hide my empties because I don't want to be a drunk Indian. I do get drunk, and I am Indian, but not both.

My mother took pictures of my father when he was passed out drunk to remind him that he was *a drunk*. Those pictures, at a time, were all I had of him.

I wonder if he ever felt this ugly, trying to exact the truth of me. A little ghost he lost. I hear empties, and I hear him. I learned to hide my bottles like him and sometimes take from the world like him. I don't think he was wrong for demanding love—it was the manner in which he asked, and whom he asked that was unforgivable.

It's strange that his ghost won't abandon me. It is the type of strange that compels me to take each bottle from my trash and consider the volume of my stomach. I want to consider what I poured into myself and how my father made a life of not remembering. I know the limit of what I can contain in each day. Each child, woman, and man should know a limit of containment. Nobody should be asked to hold more.

When I walked across the stage, I thought of you.

I believe you want my sorrow now that it is more

sophisticated, it's less contrite—less of a beggar. I'm less of a squaw. I can't entreat as well.

This story is yours, culprit of my pain. Which one of us is asking for mercy?

What do you even want with my sorrow? You are so inefficient with pain—I realized you never had to cultivate it the way I did. The way Indian women do.

You think weakness is a problem. I want to be torn apart by everything.

My people cultivated pain. In the way that god cultivated his garden, with the foresight that he could not contain or protect the life within it. Humanity was born out of pain.

I learned how to abstain from good things. I didn't expect the best things, and I have turned loss into a fortune—a personal pleasure. It's not a sustainable joy, I know. I've seen you happy. Being close to your joy has been a measured success. I've somehow retained myself, after all of this with you—retained the ability to revel in loss. This loss has spun and twisted itself into silk my sons will hold to their faces.

I almost killed myself, trying to match your potential joy. It was taking my misery. The thing I am most familiar with. The thing I rove into love. I realized that I could have you and the pain.

Pain expanded my heart. Pain brought me to you, and our children have blood memories of sorrow and your joy, too. They inherited their share, to cultivate their own children, whose humanity and gentleness will remind them of you and me.

Our boys, their compassion to will away inherited sorrow, it's what makes them good and mine and Indian.

Had I not been born and cultivated in this history, I wonder how dim and dumb my life would be. I feel fortunate with this education, and all these horrors, and you.

Today, in front of a slew of white authors, during a fellowship, with a drink in my hand, I said that I was untouchable. There was a gasp, and maybe it was a hundred years of work for my name to arrive here, where I can name my pain so well that people are afraid of the consequences and power.

11

BETTER PARTS

Mom, I won't speak to you the way we spoke before. We tried to be explicit with each other. Some knowledge can only be a song or a symbol. Language fails you and me. Some things are too large.

What of the body, Wahzinak? What of your skin— that pine, and then the winter willow beneath.

What of the hair, Wahzinak? When you cut it, was it because he touched it? That is a type of mourning, too. Or was it the manner of the touch? How much of your movements do I contribute to a lack of love or the manner of it?

There is the sentiment that love is radical, from the very radicals you walked with. They say, now, that hate is the absence of love. It's poster fodder. I follow the logic to death.

What of death, Wahzinak? It's not the absence of

something, but a new thing. I would never resurrect you, but I know your sons, my sister, and I often will you in our sleep. You told us it was dangerous to travel in our dreams. I know.

What of *your* death, Wahzinak? Was exacting hunger a type of satiation? The waist and hollow stomach in your soil—is that what you wanted? I died hungry that day. Everyone's stomachs were thrown into your cedar box—all your children, still your responsibility.

I hold my baby's head to my chest. The skin is the same as kissing a narrow stream, and even his hair feels perennial, without roots, just moving. Life is a running thing without roots for me. I'll take his stomach when I die, and throat, and he'll spend his life receiving better parts that I have not split.

Do you know the reservation received your body like Christ or the Holy Ghost or the Father?

Tsel th'í:thomé.

Tà:l

Th'í:lsometsel

Are you Perpetua in the den? Was I the infant you tore from your chest, before you walked toward the lion? Mother, can I know my inheritance now?

Is the fall of man your story, Wahzinak? Not that you were born to a green world and trespassed, but were you born into the blood? Were you the corporeal manifestation of a spirit world—your leather jacket and brown body and fist—holy?

God foreordained Eve's transgression. He didn't see *you*, though. You were stealthier than Eve. So stealthy, there is no text of you—until now. You were folklore and rumor, and there is a myth a man took, like the apple, but of your person.

If the fall was purposeful, then so are your transgressions. If there were no fall, there wouldn't have been an incarnation. To ascend there must be a dark, a descent. Is that why, Wahzinak, our fathers were prisoners? My brother doesn't talk about it. I do.

Tsel th'í:thomé.

Tà:l

Th'í:lsometsel

What of Salvador, your lover, Mother? I found his words in the underground presses and in old newspaper clips, and in photos, with brown, rotting edges. Your limbs are there, beneath his. You hadn't risen yet.

You were just there turning water into wine for men.

Salvador wrote, "Que viva Wounded Knee!" And you wrote him back. He said his best weapon was his mouth and laughed. Governor Rockefeller commuted his death sentence, and prolonged yours.

Both of your mouths, weapons. Both of you, writing from boxes. You, from your island; Sal, from a box in Attica. That's how love works for a spirit like you: a determined torture. Who could fault you? Did you come from misery?

What of your mother's body, Wahzinak? Her olive

seed and the red hill earth beneath. How many times did she hold you back from the other side of the door?

Do you know you left us hungry, Wahzinak? We exacted hunger like you. When we were children, you came home and fed me bruised bananas—was that transubstantiation? Did you see my sister's eyes, like Eve's at the gates of the garden?

"What do my eyes look like?" I asked. I couldn't see.

What of my body, Mother? Do I write from pain, like Hildegard?

What of my body and the women who've left? My citrine and the bark beneath.

When you met the serpent, who was my father, what did his eyes look like? He painted you a drum. From his box, he wrote that he could not take care of you. What provocation to a spirit like you.

Do you remember when you banished the serpent, Mom? That we all waited by the door, with weapons in our hands?

In the root of my mind, which is contained like our old house, and formed just so, I see you lying down against the concrete and my father standing above you. I walk backwards up the steps, knowing my feet like I never did. Do I forgive you both? We shine brighter in heaven. You are formless to me now. But, still, your pine and winter willow are in my body. As are my grandmother's olive seed and red hill earth.

I am leaving your body in the earth, Mother. My

words lay still like shadows on the page, but they are better than nothing. Better than your formless looming and the dead men who left you. I lament and lament the beginning until the end, where your red hands are waiting. Did you foreordain heaven before you died? Was I there on your chest, or did you hold me from the door.

ACKNOWLEDGMENTS

Endless gratitude for Seabird Island Chief and Council, Cindy Kelly, SWAIA, the Institute of American Indian Arts, Vermont Studio Center, the Lannan Foundation, and Writing by Writers for all their support and generosity.

Thank you, Emma Borges-Scott, my agent, and Harry, my editor.

Ismet Prcic (Izzy), Ramona Ausubel, Linda Hogan, Toni Jensen, Justin Torres, Pam Houston, Jon Davis, Tommy Orange, Barbara Robidoux, Viva (Gris), Elissa Washuta, and my peers at IAIA M.F.A., Low Rez, and Rudolfo, I admire you all and thank you for changing my life.

Denise Baldwin, I love you. Sisters forever. Rhonda, your love is the safest, biggest, and brightest thing. Daughter, thank you for making me go back to school, and thank you for letting me bring the baby into the classroom, and thank you to your mother, who taught me how to sew, and thank you for showing me literature.

Ovila and Guyweeyo, thank you for protecting me and taking care of me. Zena, thank you for being my sister and my blood, and for your children: Jordin, Cherish, Boon, Chubby (Trevor), Boo, and Dawson. I love you, Myka.

Isadore, Baby Casey, and Isaiah, my heart—everything good—every joy in the world. I love you.

Thank you, Cathy and David.

Casey, I fall all over myself for you, every time. My god.

All my cousins—my crazy-ass cousins, and aunties and uncles, I love you. Thank you for letting me eat at your house and cook there and thank you for every nice thing you did.

Thank you, *The Rumpus, Burrow Press Review, Carve Magazine, The Offing, BOAAT, The Butter, Yellow Medicine Review, The James Franco Review, Transmotion* for the University of Kent in Canterbury (Teddy), *The Feminist Wire, Storyscape, Juxtaprose*, and *Indian Country Today*, for your support and encouragement.

Lastly, to all my friends back home, who are women now, thank you. This is something for us.

TERESE MARIE MAILHOT is from Seabird Island Band. She graduated with an MFA from the Institute of American Indian Arts. She served as Saturday editor at *The Rumpus* and was a columnist at *Indian Country Today*. Her work appears in *West Branch*, *Guernica*, *Pacific Standard*, *Elle*, *Medium*, *BuzzFeed*, and the *Los Angeles Times*. She is the author of the *New York Times* best-selling *Heart Berries: A Memoir*. She serves as faculty at the Institute of American Indian Arts, and she's a Tecumseh Postdoctoral Fellow at Purdue University.